Exposing the Chasms in Voice Pedagogy

This concise book critically examines the intersection of power, privilege, and classical music in higher education through an extensive study of the experiences, training, and background of teachers of musical theatre singing. Mapping the divides within the voice pedagogy field, it shows how despite the growth of non-classical programmes, the teaching of vocal music in the United States continues to be structurally dominated by Western classical music. Drawing on extensive fieldwork and observations of practicing instructors, the author argues that current voice pedagogy training's classical-centred approach fails to prepare instructors to teach the range of vocal styles needed in the contemporary musical theatre profession. Combining a critical review of existing practices with proposals for change, this book sheds light on a key problem in voice pedagogy today.

Based on field research and drawing on both Shulman's signature pedagogies theory and Bourdieu's concepts of habitus, capitals, practice, and field, this book will be useful for scholars, researchers, and practitioners of voice pedagogy, higher music education, performance education, cultural studies, music, musical theatre, and theatre studies.

Dale Cox, PhD, an Australian singing teacher, researcher, and performer, is an Assistant Professor of Music at Coastal Carolina University, USA, teaching musical theatre, jazz, and all contemporary singing styles. Research interests include structural and systemic issues within the field of voice pedagogy, gender equity in academic employment, contemporary singing, cross-training classical singers into contemporary styles, and student safety in the singing studio.

Exposing the Chasms in Voice Pedagogy
Playing the Field

Dale Cox

NEW YORK AND LONDON

First published 2024
by Routledge
605 Third Avenue, New York, NY 10158

and by Routledge
4 Park Square, Milton Park, Abingdon, Oxon, OX14 4RN

Routledge is an imprint of the Taylor & Francis Group, an informa business

© 2024 Dale Cox

The right of Dale Cox to be identified as author of this work has been asserted in accordance with sections 77 and 78 of the Copyright, Designs and Patents Act 1988.

All rights reserved. No part of this book may be reprinted or reproduced or utilised in any form or by any electronic, mechanical, or other means, now known or hereafter invented, including photocopying and recording, or in any information storage or retrieval system, without permission in writing from the publishers.

Trademark notice: Product or corporate names may be trademarks or registered trademarks, and are used only for identification and explanation without intent to infringe.

ISBN: 9781032365411 (hbk)
ISBN: 9781032365442 (pbk)
ISBN: 9781003332572 (ebk)

DOI: 10.4324/9781003332572

Typeset in Times New Roman
by Newgen Publishing UK

Thank you and dedication

I couldn't have written this book without quite a few people supporting and encouraging me along the way. Thank you to Dr Melissa Forbes and Dr Andrew Hickey. Their guidance throughout my project was invaluable and I am enormously grateful for their expertise. Thank you to Dr Deborah Mulligan for making writing a book sound possible.

Thank you to my new colleagues at the Coastal Carolina University Music Department for their encouragement in the final months of writing this book.

To Maddison and Edward, thank you for your unstinting love and support. I love you both more than anything. John, thank you for the love, constant support of my adventures, for all the perfect cups of tea, and for the assistance with editing and formatting. Love you.

Lastly, but most importantly, thank you to the research participants who allowed me to come and visit you in your working lives and who trusted me with your stories.

This book is dedicated to you.

Contents

1 Marble buildings   1
   Contemporary musical theatre singing 3
   CCM singing styles 4
   How are musical theatre and CCM voice
      teachers trained? 10

2 Behind closed doors   16
   Research considerations in one-to-one singing pedagogy 16
     Orientation to research and how to read the findings 20
     The multi-sited focused ethnography 22
     Signature pedagogies, Bourdieu, and the conceptual
        framework 25

3 What was going on in musical theatre
   one-to-one singing pedagogy in universities?   33
   Where does singing teaching take place? 33
   Signature pedagogies: Mapping the content, organisation,
      and approach to one-to-one singing pedagogy 34
     Idiosyncratic approach to teaching 34
     Repertoire considerations for musical theatre
       performers 36
     Classical voice training in the musical theatre
       programme 37
     CCM training in the musical theatre programme 39
   What was missing from lessons? 43
     Amplification training 43
     Dance 45
   Why are lessons so idiosyncratic? 46

viii   Contents

4   Where did you learn to teach?   50
    Training backgrounds of musical theatre singing
       teachers 50
       What were teachers' experiences as students? 54
       Where did teachers learn musical theatre and CCM
          singing? 57
       Why does specific training matter? 63
          The specifics of voice function in CCM and musical
             theatre singing: An overview from selected research 63
          Classical singing as a deep structure in the employment
             of musical theatre singing teachers 69

5   Deep structures of voice pedagogy in
    universities in the United States   77
       The one-to-one model 77
       What can you sing? Performance backgrounds of
          musical theatre singing teachers 78
          What hadn't teachers performed? 79
          Performance practice differences between classical
             singing and contemporary singing styles 82
       How did teachers navigate the complexity of teaching
          what they are not trained to do? 83
       Notions of expertise: Performer as teacher? 85
       A complex, nuanced relationship with performance
          backgrounds 86

6   Habitus and capitals of musical theatre singing
    teachers   89
       Habitus: What is it and why does it matter? 89
          Gender 91
          Ethnicity 92
          Historic time period 93
          Culture 94
          Family background 96
          Discussion: Habitus and musical theatre voice
             pedagogy 97
       From habitus to capitals 100
       Capitals and musical theatre voice teaching 100
          Cultural capital 101
          Educational capital 104

Scientific capital 106
Symbolic capital 108
Social capital 111

7 The field of voice pedagogy 118
Field 118
Doxa and symbolic power 122
The need for civility 126
Practice: The intersection of habitus and capital within the field of musical theatre voice teaching 129

8 Turning the corner? 134
The Covid impact 134
  Gender equity, Covid, and voice pedagogy 136
Classical content in musical theatre degrees 137
The impact of not teaching CCM styles to musical theatre students 138
Impacts of classical music dominance in academia 140
Changing the field—looking forward with hope 144

Index 155

1 Marble buildings

*A student arrives at a university, excited to be admitted to the architecture programme of their choice. She is here to learn about designing and engineering buildings, about methods and materials, to be prepared and certified for professional practice. Excitedly, the student attends classes only to discover that the classes revolve around the techniques involved in creating marble buildings. These techniques have been honed over hundreds of years, creating buildings of the highest artistic and design standards. The student loves marble—it is beautiful, classic, expensive, and rare, but the student is realistic— marble buildings are a tiny percentage of the marketplace. The goal in pursuing this degree was to have a career designing and creating buildings made of materials which work best for the situation and the budget of the project. Considering marble is rarely used in building practice in the marketplace, the student approaches her professor and asks, "When do we learn about building with wood, steel, concrete, and bricks?" Her professor responds with shock: "Why would you need to learn about those materials? Design and building skills using marble have been taught for hundreds of years. Marble buildings represent the highest art form of architecture, creating the most aesthetically pleasing work. Working in marble means that you are at the pinnacle of architecture. And those who **truly** know building will understand that what you have learnt is of the highest standard". The student, shocked, asks, "But who will I design buildings for?" The professor responds, "You will build for those who appreciate true beauty. For those with the wealth, privilege, taste, and power to afford the best. And then, once you have built at least one building for the elite, you will be qualified and legitimised and able to come*

DOI: 10.4324/9781003332572-1

2 Marble buildings

back and teach marble building design practices to other students like yourself".

The above story would be considered ludicrous in real life. In many degrees specialisation comes after general knowledge. Imagine a medical student studying only foot surgery, but not anatomy and physiology of the whole body. However, I have met many teachers and performers who assumed that by doing a music performance degree they would learn how to play the music style of their choice. To an outsider a music degree sounds like it teaches you how to play, or sing, any musical style, just like an architecture degree would teach the architect how to design buildings in all manner of materials. However, in higher education many music performance degrees might be more accurately described as specialist Western classical music performance degrees. Just like the need for various types of contemporary buildings requires a variety of materials, singing different types of music requires different types of skillsets and vocal functions. It can take years of training and creative development to acquire the specific vocal skills, professionalism, and creative mindset to maintain a fulltime career as a musical theatre or Contemporary Commercial Music (CCM) performer.

CCM is a term used in voice pedagogy to refer to all kinds of contemporary singing styles, including musical theatre.[1] Throughout this book I differentiate between musical theatre singing, which has its own specific style requirements and dramatic expectations, and CCM styles which include pop, rock, R&B, jazz, country, folk, indie, and any other contemporary commercial singing styles. While specialist jazz courses have existed within music programmes for many years, and there has been recent increased demand for musical theatre degrees in the United States,[2] for many years music departments in universities in the United States have focused on teaching classical singing styles.[3] Literature reporting on conservatoire-style training of voice students continues to place classical voice training as a default, making mention of musical theatre voice training as a separate sub-section of voice teaching, with no reference at all to the field of CCM singing within the Higher Music Education (HME) environment.[4] This focus on classical singing training continues, despite documented steep declines in classical music enrolments.[5] This decline in enrolments may be related to market forces and potential career outcomes. While

HME continues to be skewed towards classical music education, total classical music consumption in America in the first half of 2019 was only 1% of total music engagement (and this includes both instrumental and vocal music) while CCM styles make up the bulk of purchased music, both by download, streaming, and in CD sales.[6] Yet within HME these contemporary styles, by their considerable absence in programme titles, have traditionally been structurally othered, marginalised, and minimised.

Contemporary musical theatre singing

The increase in musical theatre programmes is of particular interest due to the hybrid nature of musical theatre singing. While most CCM singers confine themselves to only one specific style, musical theatre performers are now expected to authentically appropriate the stylistic and functional forms of many different CCM styles, as well as the belt, legit, and mix singing required in traditional musical theatre practice.[7] Solo CCM performers may cross styles, or establish new ones, but they are rarely called upon to sing in many *different* CCM styles. Musical theatre singers must be able to sing across styles, sometimes within a single performance.[8] In this highly competitive industry, stylistic versatility produces the widest range of employment opportunities for musical theatre performers. An example of this is the character of "Rosalie Mullins" in *School of Rock*. The performer must be able to sing both a rock ballad and an adaptation of the Queen of the Night aria from Mozart's *The Magic Flute*. The character "The Lady of the Lake" in *Spamalot* must be able to sing legit, traditional Broadway belt, pop, and jazz styles.

Many singing styles found in the CCM taxonomy have been assimilated into musical theatre repertoire. One study analysed the voice styles required by musical theatre performers to audition for professional work in the United States over a six-month period. In this study, auditions included work for Broadway productions, national tours, regional and Off-Broadway productions, workshops, theme parks, and cruise ship employment opportunities.[9] Of the audition opportunities advertised, 55% were for pop/rock and other CCM genres, traditional musical theatre styles made up the remaining 45% of audition notices, and only 5% were for legit style. In 2009–2010, 72% of touring productions in the

United States required pop/rock singing.[10] A revival of *Oklahoma!* won the Tony for Revival of a Musical with a "seven-member hootenanny-style band" with "well-known melodies ... reimagined ... with the vernacular throb and straightforwardness of country and western ballads".[11] Industries which resource musical theatre performers have long accepted this shift in singing styles. For example, one online sheet music retailer provides audition cuts of CCM songs for performers requiring CCM repertoire.[12]

CCM singing styles

Each of the different CCM styles requires singers to perform in specific, identifiable ways to deliver an authentic and appropriate performance. Supporting the importance of singing with style accuracy, the National Association of Teachers of Singers (NATS) have published a series of books titled "So You Want to Sing ..." focusing on specific singing styles.[13] These titles are guides for singers interested in performing a variety of different singing styles including rock, jazz, gospel, country, folk, blues, cabaret, and musical theatre. Countering the traditional and pervasive view among many traditionally trained voice teachers that "if you can sing classical you can sing anything", the distinguished body of singing voice teachers, The American Academy of Teachers of Singing (AATS), released a position paper in 2008 stating unequivocally that classical singing is physiologically and acoustically different to CCM singing. The Academy state that "the vocal techniques required to produce those styles are not likely to be interchangeable"[14] and that teaching the diverse demands of singers and styles within CCM requires "different pedagogical approaches".[15] Further, performing contemporary styles with classical technique may be "deleterious" to vocal health.[16]

Each CCM style has its own distinct vocal requirements which are not necessarily generic to the entirety of CCM singing. It is useful for CCM teachers to understand where the commonalities and differences lie between these genres—the elements distinguishing approach, functionality, and style in CCM require "a level of specialized knowledge, training and competence by the people teaching it".[17] Table 1.1 delineates some of the specificities involved in a selection CCM singing genres. It should be noted that some of these elements of function and style intersect between

Table 1.1 Comparison of CCM function and style by genre

CCM genre	Voice functions heard	Style elements
Rock (Chandler, 2014; Edwards, 2014)	Female: mostly chest and chest mix (chest belt), medium–high pitches belted. High subglottal pressure, low–medium breath flow (harder rock and earlier female rock singers used more airflow). Male: chest, chest mix, reinforced falsetto,[a] high subglottal pressure, low–medium breath flow. Neutral to high laryngeal position.	Clean to gritty tone. Powerful singing. Intense emotional content. Unique sounds highly valued. Speech quality, not necessarily precise. Consonants at the end of words dropped. Highly rhythmic articulation. Clean, breathy, and glottal onsets and releases. Vocal fry. Closed mouth vowels for faster tempos, open mouth vowels for ballads/epic rock. Tongue position can vary from flat to high and arched forward. Diphthongs sung (vowel "morphing"). Effects—distortion, grunts, growls, creaks, cry.
Country (Garner, 2016)	Female: chest, mix, head, belting, yodel,[b] fry, whistle. Male: chest, chest mix, yodel,[b] fry. May have a slightly higher subglottal pressure due to use of belt.	Rhythmic, speech-like, conversational phrasing. Effects—fry, cry, "dip and push", fall off, breathy high notes, rich warm low notes. Vowels very bright, use of twang. Southern American vowels most common. Exaggerated use of diphthongs common. Forward "mask" placement.
Pop (Chandler, 2014)	Female: all registrations may be used, although mostly mix—both chest mix and head mix. Head register used rarely. Specialty singing in whistle register.	Short conversational phrasing. Speech-like articulation. Very rhythmic, often syncopated and linked closely to the groove of the song. Consonants at the end of words and phrases are generally de-emphasised.

(*Continued*)

Table 1.1 (Continued)

CCM genre	Voice functions heard	Style elements
	Male: chest mix, mostly head mix, head/ reinforced falsetto.[a] Larynx is neutral to raised. Very occasionally lowered. Breath flow and pressure not as great as for rock, more conversational, too much breath pressure and airflow can be damaging and cause constriction and damage. In moments of emotional intensity belt may be used and the breath pressure increased, and flow decreased accordingly.	Onsets and releases may be glottal, breathy, scooped, creaks, fry, cry, sob. Effects such as fry, creak, breathiness, growls, and grunts are also used as desired. Vowels are generally bright, although not always. Generally American accent. Individuality is highly prized. Runs (long melismas) and riffs (shorter melismas) often improvised. Subtle vibrato.
Jazz (Shapiro, 2015)	Female: chest, chest mix, head mix, head, occasionally belt. Male: chest, chest mix. Breath flow may be high (breathiness) to low (belted sounds).	Individuality highly prized. Rhythmic embellishments may be for expressive purposes or musical purposes, focus on 2 and 4 beats. Often back phrased. Internalisation of grooves such as Latin, swing, etc. important. Rubato phrasing also an important element. Vowels may be warmer, darker, or brighter, depending on the performer's choice. Free sounding tone with laid back, relaxed phrasing. Conversational delivery. Effects: growls, moans, cries. May emulate instrumentalists.

Table 1.1 (Continued)

CCM genre	Voice functions heard	Style elements
		Improvisation. Scat singing. Pitch bending, accenting specific words for emotional interpretation. Blue notes. Good "jazz ears" for harmonic chordal structure. Straight tone to vibrato (dependent on singer).
Gospel (Robinson-Martin, 2016)	Female: mostly chest, chest mix, and belting. Also head mix (brassy), occasionally head. Male: chest, chest mix, head mix, falsetto. Fry. Register flips. Registration will depend on the emotional content of the song. Breath requires efficiency with rib cage stabilisation, high sub glottal pressure, low airflow for chest dominant/belted sounds. Dynamic range from soft to very loud. Breath/vocal folds must be coordinated to maintain vocal strength and health.	Expressiveness of personal faith via voice and body. Sounds and style of singing may differ from congregation to congregation depending on cultural concerns. Individuality of soloist highly prized—reflective of faith. Speech dominant vowels: Bright and brassy to warm and dark. Most common is full bright, brassy or edgy sound. Effects: Fry, glottal attacks, breathiness, gravel onset. Nasality acceptable, especially in high registers. Gravel sounds include squalls, whoops, growls, and midvoice. Vowel distortion. Vibrato, terminal vibrato.

(*Continued*)

Table 1.1 (Continued)

CCM genre	Voice functions heard	Style elements
		Melodic improvisation requiring great vocal agility. Slides, glissandos, leans (appoggiatura), blue notes, falls, scoops, neighbour tones, passing tones, escape tones, turns, tails, runs, melodic alterations, scat, textual interpolations, ad-libbing. Rhythmic improvisations. Fermatas, shortened phrases, back phrasing, front phrasing, syncopation. Gospel "feel" 6/8, 9/8, 12/8. Tempo varies according to interpretation.
Folk (Mindel, 2016)	Female: chest, chest mix, head mix, and head. Male: chest, chest mix, head mix, falsetto.	Straight tone, close harmony. Short speech-like phrasing and articulation. Speech-like vowels. Forward, "nasal" resonance. Registration flips, yodels, and exploiting the "break". Bright vowels, many colours, not "trained" vowels, often smaller mouth shapes. "honesty, humility, introversion … not showing off" (Mindel, 2016, p. 61). Rhythmic patterns speech-like, syncopated, anticipation, and behind the beat, off-beat shuffle. Slurs.

Table 1.1 (Continued)

CCM genre	Voice functions heard	Style elements
		Melodic variations and ornamentations often improvised. Flip upwards at the end of a word. Volume stays the same (no increase or decrease in intensity). Vocal perfection is not required, authenticity and naturalness are preferred. Sometimes stillness (deadpan) facial muscles in performance.

Notes:
[a] Reinforced falsetto (men) is equivalent in function to head mix (women) (LoVetri et al., 2014, p. 63).
[b] A yodel is a functionally a quick registration flip between chest and head.

styles, and that CCM styles can merge and converge. The singer of CCM styles has the artistic freedom to live beyond a rules-based soundscape, rather than within a narrow, rules-based approach to vocal production. The information compiled in this table is based on the literature quoted and serves to illustrate the specificity of function and style within CCM styles.

Reinhert has discussed the difficulty of fitting in *everything* required of a professional CCM performer within the traditional academic structure of a four-year undergraduate degree focused on CCM singing.[18] This indicates that like classical singing, expert CCM singing requires both the in-depth and long-term training indicated by AATS.[19] If students are being trained in musical theatre singing, and musical theatre singing requires additional CCM singing styles, and these styles are being taught in universities to prepare students for professional employment, the question arises: How are singing teachers who are working with these students trained to teach these styles?

How are musical theatre and CCM voice teachers trained?

While voice pedagogy training is shifting towards an evidence-based approach,[20] learning about voice functionality and having a selection of exercises at hand to use in lessons is different to understanding *what* appropriate application is required in the lesson *when*. Voice teachers need to have an "educated ear",[21] and considerable background knowledge in physiology, anatomy, style requirements, and artistry to understand *when* to apply *what* technique. This knowledge and application of skill is often gained over years of practice in the field, through learning how to work with many individual students, and mediated through an understanding of the personality, learning style, individual goals, and background of the student. Each vocal instrument is unique and learning how to develop and "play" each voice takes skill and discernment by both the singer and the instructor. Voice pedagogy skills have traditionally been passed down through a master–apprentice approach using the one-to-one teaching model. However, the presence of graduate voice pedagogy programmes indicates a market for voice teachers to gain formal validation for their skills in what continues to be an unregulated marketplace.[22] Anyone can be a singing teacher—there are no regulations or certification requirements. This is a disturbing fact considering the application of incorrect technique has the potential to cause vocal damage requiring rehabilitation or surgery. There is also no training required in the fields of education or educational psychology to become a singing teacher. Further, degrees in vocal performance, or even general music, which might be seen by the public, music schools, or universities to qualify a person to be a singing teacher, do not always include pedagogical or educational components.

Many performers become teachers without formal training in pedagogy. However, in HME teachers are expected to be experts in their discipline. Historically, voice teachers from the music departments of universities were expected to teach music theatre voice students, and these teachers tended to be classically trained.[23] Another strategy used in HME to find faculty to teach musical theatre students is to employ musical theatre performers to teach voice, following the traditional master–apprentice pedagogical model used by classical voice teachers who may practice teaching singing alongside a performance career. While performance experience alone might have previously created access to academic employment within HME, increasingly teachers are also expected to have postgraduate qualifications. Due to a lack of CCM-focused graduate programmes in the United States, many of these qualifications are still based on classical singing performance.[24]

Finding skilled teachers in musical theatre *and* CCM genres who have the requisite qualifications in these specialised fields may prove challenging to academia.[25] Currently little is known about *how* teachers learn the required functionality and stylistic nuances of CCM singing. Previous research indicated that many teachers who teach both musical theatre and classical styles have little training or performance experience in specific CCM or musical theatre voice pedagogy.[26] The industry shift towards increased CCM genres within the musical theatre repertoire has problematised the pedagogical approach for voice teachers whose voice training and performance background may have been largely within a classical framework, yet whose daily work is to teach musical theatre singers.

While some form of graduate training is becoming the standard requirement for voice teachers at universities, many voice pedagogy programmes continue to have a classical focus and are taught by classically trained teachers.[27] DeSilva examined the number of CCM (inclusive of musical theatre) voice pedagogy programmes available for postgraduate students.[28] They noted that, to be considered for employment universities in the United States, it was standard for voice teachers to have a master's degree, and increasingly a doctorate. Master's and doctoral programmes focused on musical theatre voice pedagogy certainly exist in the United States.[29] However, at the time of writing, the only specialised programme for CCM voice pedagogy in the United States was the Master of Music in CCM Voice Pedagogy at Shenandoah University (SU). SU previously offered a Doctor of Musical Arts (DMA) programme which included CCM pedagogy and style as *part* of the programme, however prospective students needed to already have experience in classical repertoire to audition for this programme, which made it inaccessible to CCM teachers with no experience in classical voice. However, in 2020 SU launched a new DMA in CCM voice pedagogy where the requirement to sing in classical style was removed from the audition process.

If singing teachers working within the university system are educated by this same system, and universities predominately provide training in classical singing rather than CCM genres, how, in practice, are teachers managing the transition towards teaching musical theatre style and function? Further, how do these classically trained teachers use their pedagogical training when addressing the other CCM genres now required within the musical theatre industry? I was curious to discover how musical theatre singing teachers in universities in the United States applied their pedagogical tools to prepare their students to sing the variety of CCM styles required of the musical theatre industry. While I found fascinating answers to this question, the process of research exposed alarmingly regular stories of discrimination, and a problematic lack of access to appropriate academic training for the work at hand. The stories of the teachers began to expose systemic and structural issues within HME. This book is about pedagogical considerations exposed by observations of one-to-one singing lessons of research participants. But it is also about why the teachers taught the way they did, their stories, and how, as a field of industry, voice pedagogy training might move forward into a more inclusive and representative future.

Notes

1 LoVetri, 2008.
2 Edwards, 2018a.
3 Baldwin et al., 2017.
4 King & Nix, 2019.
5 Edwards, 2018b.
6 Nielson, 2019.
7 LoVetri et al., 2014.
8 LoVetri, 2013; LoVetri et al., 2014.
9 Green et al., 2014.
10 Edwards, 2018c.
11 Brantley, 2019, para. 11.
12 www.musicnotes.com/audition/
13 There are now 20 different styles covered by this series, www.nats.org/So_You_Want_To_Sing_Book_Series.html.
14 American Academy of Teachers of Singing, 2008, p. 1.
15 Ibid.
16 Bartlett, 2010.

17 Chandler, 2014, p. 35.
18 Reinhert, 2020.
19 American Academy of Teachers of Singing, 2008.
20 Ragan, 2018.
21 LoVetri et al. (2014), p. 54.
22 Rollings, 2019.
23 Boardman, 1987.
24 DeSilva, 2016.
25 DeSilva, 2016; Edwin, 2009.
26 LoVetri & Means Weekly, 2003.
27 DeSilva, 2016; Edwin, 2009; McCoy, 2014.
28 DeSilva, 2016.
29 At the time of writing, Boston Conservatory and New York University offered voice pedagogy programmes in classical and music theatre genres. Rider University offers an online Master of Voice Pedagogy and offers either a classical or Musical Theatre track. There are increasing numbers of programmes which combine classical and musical theatre pedagogy. In addition to these programmes are graduate programmes which combine classical voice pedagogy and include lab experiences and voice science, for example, the programmes at the New England Conservatory and Syracuse University. With a sole focus on musical theatre pedagogy, Penn State University offers a Master of Fine Arts in Musical Theatre Vocal Pedagogy and Carthage College offers a Master of Music in Musical Theatre Voice Pedagogy.

Outside of the United States, the Queensland Conservatorium, Griffith University offers a Master of Music Studies program where applicants can focus on CCM voice pedagogy and do not need to audition with classical style. An online Master of Arts in Voice Pedagogy program is presented by the Voice Study Centre in the UK and is accredited through the University of Wales Trinity St David. This program does not specify a stylistic focus in terms of its approach to voice pedagogy. A search of graduate voice pedagogy programmes at the time of writing did not reveal other programmes focused *solely* on CCM singing, perhaps indicating that this gap in academic provision of specialist CCM pedagogy for aspiring voice teachers may not exist exclusively in the United States.

References

American Academy of Teachers of Singing. (2008). *In support of Contemporary Commercial Music (nonclassical) voice pedagogy*. www.americanacademyofteachersofsinging.org/assets/articles/CCM VoicePedagogy.pdf

Baldwin, J., Reinhert, K., & Edwards, M. (2017, May 31–June 4). Two surveys of commercial music degree programs. In M. Edwards (Chair), *Care of the Professional Voice*. Symposium conducted at the meeting of The Voice Foundation, Philadelphia.

Bartlett, I. (2010). One size doesn't fit all: Tailored training for contemporary commercial singers. In S. Harrison (Ed.), *Perspectives on teaching singing: Australian pedagogues sing their stories* (pp. 227–243). Australian Academic Press.

Boardman, S. (1987). *Voice training for the musical theatre singer*. (Doctor of Musical Arts in Voice). Retrieved from ProQuest database. (8722053)

Brantley, B. (2019, April 7). *Review: A smashing 'Oklahoma!' is reborn in the Land of Id*. The New York Times. www.nytimes.com/2019/04/07/theater/oklahoma-review.html

Chandler, K. (2014). Teaching popular music styles. In S. Harrison & J. O'Bryan (Eds.), *Teaching singing in the 21st century* (pp. 35–51). Springer. doi: 10.1007/978-97-017-8851-9

DeSilva, B. (2016). A survey of the current state of contemporary commercial music (CCM) vocal pedagogy training at the graduate level. (Publication no. 10111351) [Doctor of Musical Arts Dissertation]. ProQuest.

Edwards, M. (2014). *So you want to sing Rock 'n' Roll: A guide for professionals*. Rowman & Littlefield.

Edwards, M. (2018a, March 13). *Music Theatre* [web page]. https://auditioningforcollege.com/schools/musical-theatre/

Edwards, M. (2018b). Why it's time to add CCM to your studio. In M. Hoch (Ed.), *So you want to sing CCM? (Contemporary Commercial Music): A guide for performers* (pp. 264–286). Rowman & Littlefield.

Edwards, M. (2018c, March 13). *The truth about pop/rock musicals* [web log]. https://auditioningforcollege.com/musical-theatre/the-truth-about-poprock-musicals/

Edwin, R. (2009). What's going on on Broadway? *Journal of Singing*, 66(1), 71–73.

Garner, K. K. (2016). *So You Want to Sing Country: A Guide for Performers*. Rowman & Littlefield.

Green, K., Freeman, W., Edwards, M., & Meyer, D. (2014). Trends in musical theatre voice: An analysis of audition requirements for singers. *Journal of Voice, 28*(3), 324–327. doi: 10.1016/j.jvoice.2013.10.007

King, M., & Nix, J. (2019). Conservatory teaching and learning. In G. Welch, D. Howard, & J. Nix (Eds.) *The Oxford handbook of singing* (pp. 689–705). Oxford University Press.

LoVetri, J. (2008). Contemporary commercial music. *Journal of Voice, 22*(3), 260–262.

LoVetri, J., & Means Weekly, E. (2003). Contemporary commercial music (CCM) survey: Who's teaching what in nonclassical music. *Journal of Voice, 17*(2), 207–215. doi: 10.1016/S0892-1997(03)00004-3

LoVetri, J. (2013). The necessity of using functional training in the independent studio. *Journal of Singing, 70*(1), 79–86.

LoVetri, J., Saunders-Barton, M., & Means Weekly, E. (2014). A brief overview of approaches to teaching the music theatre song. In S. Harrison & J. O'Bryan (Eds.), *Teaching singing in the 21st century* (pp. 53–66). Springer. doi: 10.1007/978-97-017-8851-9

McCoy, S. (2014). Singing pedagogy in the twenty-first century: A look toward the future. In S. Harrison & J. O'Bryan (Eds.), *Teaching singing in the 21st century* (pp. 13–20). Springer. doi: 10.1007/978-97-017-8851-9

Mindel, V. (2016). *So You Want to Sing Folk Music: A Guide for Performers.* Rowman & Littlefield.

Nielson, (2019). *Nielson mid-year report US 2019.* Retrieved from www.nielsen.com/wp-content/uploads/sites/3/2019/06/nielsen-us-music-mid-year-report-2019.pdf

Ragan, K. (2018). Defining evidence-based pedagogy: A new framework. *Journal of Singing, 75*(2), 157–160.

Reinhert, K. (January 20, 2020). *Expanding the circle: CCM and popular music in higher ed.* https://singinginpopularmusics.com/2020/01/27/expanding-the-circle-ccm-and-popular-music-in-higher-ed/

Robinson-Martin, T. (2016). *So You Want to Sing Gospel: A Guide for Performers.* Rowman & Littlefield.

Rollings, A. (2019). Of charlatans, humbugs, and pocketbooks: Advocacy of standards, education, and certification for voice teachers in The Bulletin of the National Association of Teachers of Singing, 1944–1954. *Voice and Speech Review, 14*(1), 1–19. doi: 10.1080/23268263.2020.1684630

Shapiro, J. (2015). *So You Want to Sing Jazz: A Guide for Professionals.* Rowman & Littlefield.

2   Behind closed doors

Research considerations in one-to-one singing pedagogy

Before I discuss the ideas generated by this research about teaching practices and the field of voice pedagogy, it is important to state how this research was done, and why it was done using the selected research design. The research method used in this project was novel to the field of one-to-one voice pedagogy research, therefore the development process of the research requires explanation.[1]

When I started my research, I wanted to understand what was being taught to musical theatre singing students in their lessons. I wanted to discover the content of lessons, the way the content was structured in the time frame of the lesson, and the pedagogical practices teachers used to deliver this content. Further I was interested in *why* teachers delivered their lessons in the way they did. I wanted to be "a fly on the wall", to see and hear in real time what was happening behind the closed doors[2] of one-to-one singing lessons. However, as a singing teacher myself, I was sensitive to the potential impact on lessons of a researcher's presence in the teaching space during a lesson. It is not unreasonable to assume that teachers might feel uncomfortable having a researcher observing their teaching practices. Further, the change in the usual teaching dynamic could result in altered teaching behaviour to suit an audience. Working out how I could achieve my research goals within the private space[3] of the one-to-one singing lesson required thoughtful planning.

Previous research into one-to-one music teaching has demonstrated participant discomfort with in-person observational methods, particularly if participants believe their teaching

DOI: 10.4324/9781003332572-2

effectiveness is being examined.[4] My previous experience as a teacher meant I understood the nature of learning singing and the potential discomfort of participant teachers. Training breakthroughs and observable changes in a singing student may happen over a long period of time, longer than I expected to be able to conduct field observations. I was also sensitive to my own position—while I am an experienced voice teacher with graduate qualifications, I did not feel it was appropriate to judge the effectiveness of another teacher's practices within the relatively short time frame at each location considered viable within the overall time frame and within financial constraints of the research. There is no published rubric established within the singing discipline for one-to-one teacher evaluation. Further, teaching effectiveness in singing is notoriously difficult to measure. Effectiveness might be judged by professional employment, by observed change over a certain period, or by some kind of scientific measurement of singing processes. It might be considered successful by evaluating the long-term vocal health of singers, by their ability to perform without obvious "faults", or by examining the emotional wellbeing of the student during their time with a teacher. Measuring teaching effectiveness in singing teaching is highly subjective and difficult to measure. Teaching effectiveness was **not** the object of this research.[5]

Because of the difficulty surrounding the question of effectiveness, the research questions were carefully framed to focus on reporting the observed practices of lessons (content and structure) within the academic context. To understand more deeply the context of a teacher's practices, the research also focused on the performance background and the academic training of teachers. The research questions which guided the project were:

- How do musical theatre singing teachers apply their pedagogical skills during voice lessons?
- How do musical theatre singing teachers differentiate the various functions and styles within CCM singing genres for musical theatre students?
- How do musical theatre singing teachers trained in CCM apply their practice?
- How has the educational background of musical theatre singing teachers assisted them in their work?

Once the research focus was established, I needed to find participants willing to have me visit their institutions, to be observed during their normal practice, and to answer my questions. Gaining agreement from potential participants was vital. Earlier research into one-to-one pedagogy by researchers has met with participant resistance.[6] Aside from the above concerns regarding effectiveness and researcher judgement, other considerations might influence participant sensitivity to a researcher's presence during a lesson. Many singing teachers begin working without formal education qualifications or experience.[7] In lieu of qualifications, music teachers report that the main influence informing their teaching practice is their own previous experiences of private lessons.[8] Previous researchers with access to one-to-one singing studios have been employees of the conservatory or university providing the singing lessons. This employment granted automatic "insider" status to researchers and provided credibility and a sense of safety for participants.[9]

Previous insider-based one-to-one pedagogy research considered participant sensitivity when selecting data collection tools. This has resulted in indirect (to the moment of the lesson) data collection methods including interviews, focus groups, and video data.[10] However, I was interested in being present in the moment of the lesson. I wanted to be able to hear the acoustic properties of the singing as it was happening and be able to ask questions (almost) in the moment of the teaching. As an experienced singing teacher, I was aware of the importance of the relational nature of one-to-one singing lessons. I was also aware that singing teachers themselves are often working in isolation, and that a relational approach to researching this type of pedagogy might provide information for my research which would not necessarily be disclosed in a more formal interview setting where there was no pre-existing relationship with the interviewer. I believed that a relationship of trust with teacher participants would be important. This trust would possibly create an environment where open, non-defensive pedagogical discussions about what was happening in the moment of the lesson could occur. In addition to casual and impromptu conversations, I was interested in discovering participant opinions and feelings regarding their own training and background, especially in relation to what they were teaching. This information can be difficult to obtain.

In voice pedagogy interview-based literature, lineage is perceived as providing validation to a teacher's practice due to the traditional master–apprentice approach to singing training. Singing teachers, particularly those who have come from highly visible performance careers, are often connectors to industry for students. Teachers may provide networking opportunities which can lead to career success, and these connections can be considered more valuable than the actual pedagogical skill of the teacher in question for a potential professional performer. Valourising of teachers is usual practice in voice pedagogy literature, and the status of a teacher can exert a powerful influence over a student. I was interested in whether the condition of anonymity might yield important information regarding training and background of the teachers. I knew that this potential data, which might be negative, could not be revealed and published if it was not anonymised due to fear of retaliation, reputational damage, ostracism, or legal ramifications.

When I was considering the type of data I wanted to collect, I realised that I was interested in both interview data and an observation period of teacher practices. I was interested in interviewing my participants *after* trying to understand their practices of teaching through this observation and casual conversation. I believed that I needed more than a day's observation in the field for teachers to feel comfortable and to teach in their usual manner while having me in the room as they taught lessons[11] because behaviours "are more stable over time than attitudes and opinions"[12] and there is often a "gap between what we say and what we do, between what people think and feel and what they do, between behaviour and attitude, between sentiments and acts".[13] Choosing field research meant that the interview data of teacher opinions, backgrounds, and training could be viewed in the context of the observational data of actually taught lessons within a specific moment in time.

By selecting field research as a methodological approach, I entered into a "Big Q", or fully qualitative research framework.[14] This type of research emphasises "both qualitative techniques and philosophy".[15] Big Q research also requires explicit discussion of the philosophical orientations underpinning the project. This is required to demonstrate both quality assurance and research coherence.[16]

Orientation to research and how to read the findings

The following section is offered as an interpretive framework through which to consider the discussions contained in this book.[17] The disclosure of an interpretive framework is usually not provided in voice pedagogy literature; however, it is essential for understanding the context through which to view the contents of this book. By providing the following information, I hope to provide those unfamiliar with this type of research within the voice pedagogy field a way to consider the valuable insights Big Q research can provide the discipline.

This book is based on an ontological position regarding the nature of reality as being multiple and dependant on the individual. As a researcher I have a concept of reality which may be different to my participants', and in turn to yours as a reader. This orientation asserts that multiple realities can co-exist based upon subjective experience. The ability to hold reality as different for different people in different contexts, for both myself as participant-researcher and for my participant teachers, recognises a multiplicity of viewpoints, which may be contradictory and complex in nature. The inclusion of multiple realities reflects a depth of understanding and inclusiveness regarding the intricacies involved in the research. It acknowledges the expertise of participants and the fact that individuals acquire and demonstrate this expertise in various ways. Fundamental to this project was the assumption that vocal pedagogy and what constitutes reality in the field of vocal pedagogy is complex, nuanced, and individual to the person practicing teaching. This orientation to reality allows for the stories of the participants to be heard and included, providing a richness to the project which is both personal and specific to the context of this study.

This research also assumes a constructionist epistemology. Constructionism is an approach to research that emphasises that "meaning" is a mental construct which may be multiple in nature, is based on individual experiences and history, and is created through human social interaction and engagement.[18] The generation of meaning is as a social phenomenon, location and time specific,[19] which shapes the action (or inaction) of practices.[20] This epistemological position assumes that the meanings of the pedagogical experiences and ideas of singing teachers that I sought to understand are multiple. Meaning is constructed, or created, by the teachers through their experiences and history in musical theatre training, performance, and teaching, via interactions and engagements with their own teachers, colleagues, and students.

In addition to these epistemological and ontological positions, the axiology, or role of values in the research requires acknowledgement. My own values, biases, and long-held beliefs were challenged throughout this project, requiring extensive self-reflection. My own concepts of reality and knowledge required consideration, as I positioned myself as the person firmly at the centre of the research. This impacted every part of the research design, from the selection of subject matter and the research questions to decisions regarding methodology, how to collect data, how to analyse data, and what conceptual framework I applied to the data to determine my research conclusions.

The above statements of research orientations align this study with the concept of a "cohesive" approach to research.[21] "Big Q",[22] or fully qualitative research, requires this cohesive approach, from the explanation of the "big theory" of epistemological and ontological orientation to the decisions surrounding the selection of methodology and data collection and analysis methods. It further requires the use of "small theory" in the analysis process, and clear explanation of how processes and procedures were selected and used.[23] I have provided details of theory and methods here for a distinct purpose. Much of what is published in voice pedagogy research neglects this explicit statement of research orientation causing significant debate and misunderstandings among singing teachers in pedagogical forums. This provision is important due to the types of research approaches more usually found in the literature on both voice pedagogy and approaches to the one-to-one singing studio.

As scientific knowledge and understanding within voice pedagogy has expanded over the past 20 years, positivist-oriented researchers have increasingly used science-based, quantitative approaches to investigate the processes of singing.[24] The opposite extreme is commonly found in industry-based literature concerned with the aesthetic philosophic tradition which focuses on musicality or reporting of teaching practices.[25] This type of literature consists of largely uncritical reporting of information sourced from interviews, opinion pieces, or self-reporting of practices.[26]

There is also research reporting teaching practices which is a type of qualitative research known as "small q" research, that is, qualitative research done with a positivist mindset. This type of research involves the gathering of qualitative data through means such as open-ended questions within a set research design structure, using the data collected to test an initial hypothesis.[27]

I was interested in something different. I wanted the teachers to be anonymised to give them the freedom to talk about their experiences, especially if their training was not fit for purpose, without having to consider potential recriminations or a sense of disloyalty to their past teachers. This approach has proven problematic for some in the voice pedagogy community, with the commentary that naming participants would give this research credibility. This kind of critique implies that those teachers who are doing the work of teaching, but who are not "famous", or who do not have famous students, are not worthy of study. I was not interested in a large number of teachers as participants, or famous teachers who would give the work "credibility" in the eyes of the network of voice pedagogy teachers who already command influence over the field of voice pedagogy either through publications or the advertising of their famous students. I was not interested in validating few set questions, or having numerical statistics to back up my data, but in rich thick description from in-depth conversations with teachers about their experiences, practices, and philosophies.

The multi-sited focused ethnography

Because I wanted to do observations of lessons and semi-structured interviews, I conducted a multi-sited focused ethnography (MSFE).[28] While ethnography usually involves long-term field research, usually for a time period of a year or more,[29] focused ethnography has been used in specialised fields for short periods of time where the researcher has "implicit and explicit background knowledge"[30] of the field under study. This insider knowledge means that the researcher can observe events and practices for a shorter duration of time because there is an existing understanding about the nature of what is being observed. The nature of MSFE means that the researcher can follow a specific cultural group or process across multiple sites. I knew that a year in the field, the normal length of time for field research, was unviable. This period of time would be an imposition on potential participants and students and was financially unviable.

The selection of MSFE resulted in a research design where I visited six university musical theatre programmes in the United States over the 2018–2019 academic year for two weeks each. During each field visit I observed one-to-one singing lessons in the context of the academic programme and engaged in participant observation.[31] Participant observation has a long tradition in qualitative field research and requires the researcher to be present and active in the moment of data collection. This type of research involves the principal of reciprocity. In this study, reciprocity meant that I was able to contribute to the teaching environment under observation in a variety of ways. Reciprocal activities included team teaching, conducting masterclasses, providing peer reviews, and by teaching of participant teachers singing lessons.[32]

Data collection involved observations of singing lessons, site observations, semi-structured interviews with participants, and videoed lessons. All data collected was transcribed. Data analysis then proceeded using Reflective Thematic Analysis[33]. This type of analysis requires the engagement with theory throughout the analytic processes and I initially used an analytic framework based on Shulman's concept of *signature pedagogies*[34]. Signature pedagogies investigates how a pedagogy operates by identifying the surface, implicit, and deep structures of a teaching process. In addition to identifying what is in a pedagogy, signature pedagogies also investigate what might be missing from a pedagogy.

While I found signature pedagogies to be a useful framework to use during data analysis, it did not provide a framework for a deeper understanding of *why* specific pedagogical concepts, actions, or approaches might be included or missing from the observed pedagogy. It became clear to me that I would need to engage with additional theoretical approaches. After reading various philosophical and theoretical approaches,[35] I connected with Bourdieu's concepts of habitus, capitals, and practice.[36] These concepts were useful tools to engage during the analytical process by providing a framework to help explain why observed pedagogical practices were conducted in way they were, why certain aspects of the pedagogy were missing, and to delineate the pedagogical field.

Table 2.1 Data type and volume collected at each participant site

	University G	University T	University X	University Q	University M	University V
Number of teachers observed	2	2	2	3	1	3
Interview duration[a]	1:11:46	1:10:35	1:01:29	1:05:08	1:34:57	54:50
Interview transcription (words)	10,713	14,587	10,442	10,754	16,520	8,699
Lesson video duration[a]	0:58:53	0:45:23	1:06:15	0:46:40	0:45:24	0:57:36
Lesson video transcription (words)	8,133	9,205	9,313	4,597	6,508	6,716
Observations lessons (words)	19,241	12,379	13,700	19,858	15,714	12,354
General observations[b] (words)	4,238	4,871	4,256	6,679	2,931	3,443

Notes:
[a] Duration shown in hours:minutes:seconds.
[b] In addition to the above tabled data, my reflexive data across site visits constituted 28,251 words which was added to the data for analysis.

To begin to answer my initial research question of how singing teachers approached CCM styles, I mapped the content and structure of 193 one-to-one lessons. While reporting on numbers was not the goal of this research, I have provided some numerical details of the research in Table 2.1 for those readers who are interested.

I then analysed this data, combined it with the data from the interviews and videoed lessons through the lens of the conceptual framework to consider what might happening for these teachers in this spaces and times, and how this might have wider implications in the voice pedagogy field.

Signature pedagogies, Bourdieu, and the conceptual framework

The research questions framing this study were concerned with the ways musical theatre voice teachers use pedagogical skills to teach singing and sought to understand the relationship between the backgrounds and training of these teachers with their practice. Shulman's theory of signature pedagogies was used to identify the structures of the practice that constitutes musical theatre voice pedagogy, as observed in a selection of university programmes in the United States. Attention was given to what is "included", and perhaps more pertinently to this study, what was "excluded" in this practice. By using Shulman's work in this way, this project examined what constitutes the existing "signatures" of musical theatre voice pedagogy and the way that these work to shape the field. From this point the project used the theoretical concepts of Bourdieu to understand the relationships between capitals, habitus, and field (see Figure 2.1) in the generation of practices outlined through the identification of the signature pedagogies of musical theatre voice pedagogy. This project specifically explored the position of musical theatre, and through this, CCM voice pedagogy, in relation to the wider field of general voice pedagogy in academia. The conceptual framework employed in this study utilised both theories.

The identification of the *signature pedagogies* is not equivalent to Bourdieu's concept of field, but related to it through the implicit, deep, and surface structures. Signature pedagogies is a theory which can be applied to a discipline, or field, while Bourdieu's concept of field is a symbolically accepted social structure in which members

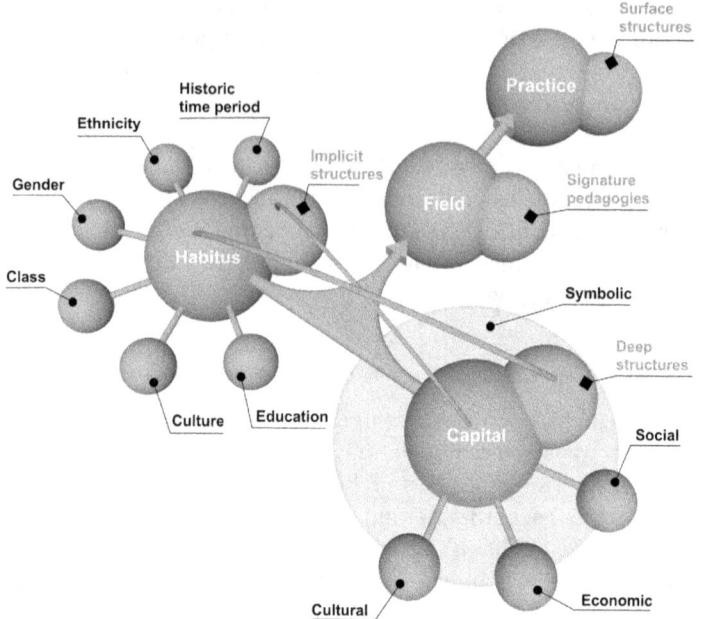

Figure 2.1 Conceptual framework: The intersection of Shulman's signature pedagogies and Bourdieu's theories of habitus, capitals, field, and practice.

position themselves according to capitals and habitus. The theory of signature pedagogies can be used to identify the surface, deep, and implicit structures within a discipline, to explain the "how" of a pedagogy. Bourdieu uses concepts of habitus and capital to explain the relative positions within the *social* structures of a field, to explain why a field is organised in the way that it is, the "why" of a field. In the context of this study Bourdieu's concepts were used to expand from signature pedagogies and the structures of the pedagogical practices observed, to explain the organisation of the field of vocal pedagogy and the positioning of musical theatre and CCM singing within it.

Using Bourdieu's theory, it is the relative amounts of capital and habitus that manifest the field, and this manifestation of field generates practice. A field has a hierarchical structure where position is determined by volume, composition, and trajectory of capitals combined with habitus. This structured positioning is always relative to other groups and individuals within the field. Taste is essential to this positioning and there is "a distinction of taste between those whose tastes are regarded as 'noble' because they have been organized and legitimated by the educational system, and those whose tastes, lacking such markers of nobility, are accorded a more lowly status".[37] The interconnection of "class-based principles ... (organize) the cultural values and practices though which classes organize, symbolize and enact their differences from one another".[38] Taste is reflective of class, and the tastes generated through habitus and field classify and organise the field.

Taste within music is a strong signifier of belonging or exclusion. What music styles are legitimised through education and therefore afforded attention through research can organise a field. An example of this is jazz music within the larger music field. Jazz might be enjoyed by those who consider themselves classically trained but who do not understand the social field of jazz music. For example, when experiencing a jazz performance, those same individuals who understand the complexities and nuances of taste and when experiencing classical music (one does not speak, one observes and pays attention to the music, one listens closely and saves all applause for the end of a performance) may think nothing of continuing a conversation throughout a jazz musician's improvisation in the middle of a song when a performance occurs outside of a formal recital hall, for example, in a restaurant or bar. Those knowledgeable in jazz as a social structure would understand that the improvisation is expected to be respected through careful attention, and then applauded at the end of the improvised section. Those who understand the jazz field would understand this within the norms of jazz performance, and those who do not, through this demonstration of their taste, denote themselves as outsiders to the social field of jazz.

A field is a social structure which requires capitals (combined with habitus) to explain the distinctions between members. If a field is a socially mediated and constructed structure, any setting within which a discipline is organised to teach or reproduce itself will constitute a field. Whether the pedagogical field is the teaching of law, medicine, architecture, or music, or indeed, voice pedagogy, the field contains social structures made up of educators operating within that field. Shulman designates the deep structures of a signature pedagogy as those assumptions about the best ways to impart knowledge to the next generation within a field. These assumptions are made by those within the social structure of a pedagogy with the ability to exert reproductive power over the rest of the field. However, these structures are invisible to those outside of the field—who are not players on the field of the pedagogical "game". This book will consider how the game of the voice pedagogy field is structured and how those within the field, playing the game, situate and structure themselves and how they are situated within the field by those in positions of authority.

Notes

1. See also Cox and Forbes (2022).
2. Carey & Grant, 2015, p. 6.
3. One-to-one pedagogy has been described as shrouded in "secrecy" (Davidson & Jordan, 2007, p. 730), inherently isolated (Burwell, 2005), and done in a "secret space" (O'Bryan & Harrison, 2014, p. 7).
4. See Persson (1994, 1996) and L'Hommedieu (1992), for examples of participant non-compliance and distrust.
5. Clear communication of the focus of the research assisted with teacher's participation in the research.
6. Persson, 1994, 1996.
7. Ibid.; Rollings, 2019.
8. Daniel & Parkes, 2017.
9. E.g., Gaunt, 2008, 2009, 2011; O'Bryan, 2014.
10. Burwell, 2006; Gaunt, 2008, 2009; O'Bryan, 2014.
11. During the preparation for starting the PhD I had visited one institution for a day to observe practices. I was viewed as an outsider. I quickly realised that I didn't have the teacher's trust to ask the questions of their practice that I wanted to ask—I needed a relationship with teachers for them to trust me.
12. Silverman, 2016, p. 115.
13. Gobo, 2008, p. 6.
14. Kidder & Fine, 1987; Braun & Clarke, 2022, p. 283.
15. Braun & Clarke, 2020, p. 283.
16. Braun & Clarke, 2022.
17. Creswell, 2014.
18. Lincoln & Guba, 1994; Lincoln et al., 2018.
19. Crotty, 1998.

20 Guba & Lincoln, 2005.
21 Braun & Clarke, 2022.
22 Kidder & Fine, 1987.
23 Braun & Clarke, 2022, 2020; Clarke, 2021.
24 E.g., Björkner, 2006; Fornhammar et al., 2020; Herbst et al., 2015; Kirsh et al., 2017; Sundberg, 1993; Sundberg et al., 2021; Titze & Sundberg, 1992.
25 Kallio, 2021.
26 For example, Benson, 2020; Blades-Zeller, 2002; Forbes, 2018, 2020; Holmes, 2020, 2021; Naismith, 2022.
27 Kidder & Fine, 1987.
28 Cox & Forbes, 2022.
29 Creswell, 2014; Silverman, 2016.
30 Knoblauch, 2005, para. 6.
31 Cox & Forbes, 2022.
32 I am forever grateful to my generous participants who so graciously allowed me to sit in their studios, taking notes, and asking questions. Without their support the project which underpins the book would have been impossible.
33 Braun & Clarke, 2006, 2020, 2022.
34 Shulman, 2005.
35 And here I must thank my supervisors, Dr Melissa Forbes and Assoc. Prof. Andrew Hickey who steered me through a minefield of wailing at the moon and gnashing of teeth as I engaged with various philosophical approaches.
36 Bourdieu, 1979/2010.
37 Ibid., pp. xix–xx.
38 Ibid., p. xx.

References

Bennett, T. (2010). Introduction to the Routledge Classics Edition. In P. Bourdieu *Distinction: A social critique of the judgement of taste* (R. Nice, Trans) (pp. xvii–xxiii). Routledge. (Original work published 1979).

Benson, E. (2020). *Training contemporary commercial singers*. Compton.

Björkner, E. (2006). Musical theatre and opera singing—Why so different? A study of subglottal pressure, voice source and formant frequency characteristics. *Journal of Voice, 22*(5), 533–540.

Blades-Zeller, E. (2002). *A spectrum of voices: Prominent American voice teachers discuss the teaching of singing*. Scarecrow.

Bourdieu, P. (2010). *Distinction: A social critique of the judgement of taste* (R. Nice, Trans). Routledge. (Original work published 1979).

Braun, V., & Clarke, V. (2006). Using thematic analysis in psychology. *Qualitative Research in Psychology, 3*, 77–101.

Braun, V., & Clarke, V. (2020). One size fits all? What counts as quality practice in (reflexive) thematic analysis. *Qualitative Research in Psychology.* doi: 10.1080/14780887.2020.1769238

Braun, V., & Clarke, V. (2022). *Thematic analysis: A practical guide.* SAGE.

Burwell, K. 2005. A degree of independence: Teachers' approaches to instrumental tuition in a University College." *British Journal of Music Education* 22(3): 199–215. doi:10.1017/S0265051705006601

Burwell, K. (2006). On musicians and singers. An investigation of different approaches taken by vocal and instrumental teachers in higher education. *Music Education Research, 8*(3), 331–347.

Carey, G., & Grant, C. (2015). Teacher and student perspectives on one-to-one pedagogy: Practices and possibilities. *British Journal of Music Education, 32*(1), 5–22. doi: 10.1017/S0265051714000084

Clarke, V. (2021). Navigating the messy swamp of qualitative research: Are generic reporting standards the answer? *Qualitative Research in Psychology.* doi: 10.1080/14780887.2021.1995555

Cox D., & Forbes, M. (2022). Introducing multi-sited focused ethnography for researching one-to-one (singing voice) pedagogy in higher education. *Music Education Research.* doi: 10.1080/14613808.2022.2138842

Creswell, J. (2014). *Research design.* SAGE.

Crotty, M. (1998). *The foundations of social research: Meaning and perspective in the research process.* Allen & Unwin.

Daniel, R., & Parkes, K. (2017). Music instrumental teachers in higher education: An investigation of the key influences on how they teach in the studio. *International Journal of Teaching and Learning in Higher Education, 29*(1), 33–46.

Davidson, J., & Jordan, N. (2007). "Private teaching, private learning": An exploration of music instrument learning in the private studio of junior and senior conservatories. In L. Bresler (Ed.), *International handbook of research in arts education* (pp. 729–754). Springer.

Forbes, M. (2018) A tale of two pedagogues: A cross-continental conversation on CCM. *Journal of Singing, 74*(5), 579–584.

Forbes, M. (2020). The soul of the voice: A conversation with Trineice Martin-Robinson. *Journal of Singing, 77*(2), 273–279.

Fornhammar, L., Sundberg, J., Fuchs, M., & Pieper, L. (2020). Measuring voice effects of vibrato-free and ingressive singing: A study of phonation threshold pressures. *Journal of Voice, 36*(4):479–486. doi: 10.1016/j.jvoice.2020.07.023

Gaunt, H. (2008). One-to-one tuition in a conservatoire: The perceptions of instrumental and vocal teachers. *Psychology of Music, 36*(2), 215–245.

Gaunt, H. (2009). One-to-one tuition in a conservatoire: The perceptions of instrumental and vocal students. *Psychology of Music, 38*(2), 178–208. doi: 10.1177/0305735609339467

Gaunt, H. (2011). Understanding the one-to-one relationship in instrumental/vocal tuition in Higher Education: comparing student and teacher perceptions. *British Journal of Music Education, 28*(2), 159–179.

Gobo, G. (2008). *Doing ethnography*. SAGE.

Guba, E. G., & Lincoln, Y. S. (2005). Paradigmatic controversies, contradictions, and emerging confluences. In N. K. Denzin & Y. S. Lincoln (Eds.), *The SAGE handbook of qualitative research* (pp. 191–215). SAGE.

Herbst, C. T., Hess, M., Müller, F., Svec, J., & Sundberg, J. (2015). Glottal adduction and subglottal pressure in singing. *Journal of Voice, 29*(4), 391–402. doi: 10.1016/j.jvoice.2014.08.009

Holmes, L. (2020). The vocal point. A conversation with Richard Miller. *Journal of Singing, 76*(4), 483–488.

Holmes, L. (2021). A conversation with Kate Lindsay: Part 1. *Journal of Singing, 77*(5), 717–721.

Kallio, A. (2021). Doing dirty work: Listening for ignorance among the ruins of reflexivity in music education research. In A. Kallio, H. Westerlund, S. Karlsen, K. Marsh, & E. Sæther (Eds.) *The politics of diversity in music education, landscapes: The arts, aesthetics, and education* (pp. 53–67). doi: 10.1007/978-3-030-65617-1_5

Kidder, L., & Fine, M. (1987). Qualitative and quantitative methods: When stories converge. *New Directions for Program Evaluation, 35*, 57–75. doi: 10.1002/ev.1459

Kirsh, E., Zacharias, S., de Alarcorn, A., Deliyski, D., Tabangin, M., & Khosla, S. (2015). Vertical phase difference and glottal efficiency in musical theatre and opera singers. *Journal of Voice, 31*(1), 130.e119–130.e125.

Knoblauch, H. (2005). Focused Ethnography. *Forum: Qualitative Social Research, 6*(3): Art. 44. http://nbn-resolving.de/urn:nbn:de:0114-fqs0503440

L'Hommedieu, R. (1992). *The management of selected educational process variables by master studio teachers in music performance,* (Publication no. 9229948) [Doctoral dissertation, Northwestern University]. Proquest.

Lincoln, Y. S., & Guba, E. G. (1994). Competing paradigms in qualitative research. In N. K. Denzin & Y. S. Lincoln (Eds.), *Handbook of qualitative research* (pp. 105–117). SAGE.

Lincoln, Yvonna S., Lynholm, S. A., & Guba E. G. (2018). Paradigmatic controversies, contradictions and emerging confluences, revisited. In N. K. Denzin & Y. S. Lincoln (Eds.), *The Sage handbook of qualitative research* (pp. 193–215). 5th Edition. SAGE.

Naismith, M. (2022). *Singing contemporary commercial music styles.* Compton.

O'Bryan, J. (2014). Habits of the mind, hand and heart: Approaches to classical singing training. In S. Harrison & J. O'Bryan (Eds.), *Teaching singing in the 21st century* (pp. 31–34). Springer. doi: 10.1007/978-97-017-8851-9

O'Bryan, J., & Harrison, S. (2014). Prelude: Positioning singing pedagogy in the twenty-first century. In S. Harrison & J. O'Bryan (Eds.), *Teaching singing in the 21st century* (pp. 1–9). Springer. doi: 10.1007/978-97-017-8851-9

Persson, R. (1994). Concert musicians as teachers: On good intentions falling short. *European Journal for High Ability, 5*(1), 79–91. doi: 10.1080/0937445940050108

Persson, R. (1996). Studying with a musical maestro: A case study of commonsense teaching in artistic training. *Creativity Research Journal, 9*(1), 33–46.

Rollings, A. (2019). Of charlatans, humbugs, and pocketbooks: Advocacy of standards, education, and certification for voice teachers in The Bulletin of the National Association of Teachers of Singing, 1944–1954. *Voice and Speech Review*, 1–19. doi: 10.1080/23268263.2020.1684630

Shulman, L. (2005). Signature pedagogies in the professions. *Daedalus, 134*(3), 52–59.

Silverman, D. (2016). *Qualitative research.* SAGE.

Sundberg, J. (1993). Breathing behavior during singing. *Journal of Singing, 49*(3), 4–51.

Sundberg, J., Salomão, G., & Scherer, K. (2021). Analyzing emotion expression in singing via Flow Glottograms, Long-Term-Average Spectra, and Expert Listener Evaluation. *Journal of Voice, 35*(1), 52–60.

Titze, I., & Sundberg, J. (1992). Vocal intensity in speakers and singers. *Journal Acoustical Society of America, 91*(5), 2936–2946.

3 What was going on in musical theatre one-to-one singing pedagogy in universities?

Initially I set out to examine what the signature pedagogies were of musical theatre singing voice lessons in the one-to-one context. Previously Don et al. identified the signatures of the one-to-one music performance lesson in higher music education using Shulman's conceptual framework.[1] They describe the goals of these lessons as the attainment of musical expression and technical facility through a weekly lesson with a teacher who is both skilled at performance and teaching. Approaches to teaching were noted as including critique, modelling, imagery, coaching, and explanation. The authors note that applied music study uses "the standard repertoire of the individual instrument, complemented by exercises such as scales and arpeggios".[2] While at a surface level these teaching practices were confirmed by my research, there were some notable variables which only became evident through observing multiple teachers, over multiple lessons, in multiple spaces and times. Through mapping the practices of teachers, I identified what Shulman calls the *surface structures* of musical theatre voice pedagogy. Surface structures are the "concrete, operational acts of teaching and learning".[3]

Where does singing teaching take place?

The private, one-to-one nature of the musical theatre voice studio environment was customary, although it should be noted that in many lessons this dynamic changed not only by having me as a researcher in the room, but by the presence of an accompanist, and by some lessons being conducted with two students, one

DOI: 10.4324/9781003332572-3

teacher, and one accompanist. All lessons were held in the teacher's domain, a teaching space which was also the office of the participant teacher. This is a considerably different teaching location to other types of training provided in musical theatre programmes—dance and acting are generally taught in a classroom/studio environment with peers. However, private one-to-one teaching is the usual mode of teaching instrumentalists and singers in HME. The teaching of singers in musical theatre programmes began with teachers drawn from music departments[4] and so has continued to use this model.

The private teaching space was often dominated by the teacher's educational qualifications, performance posters, scientific posters of the vocal instrument, pedagogy textbooks, sheet music, and scores. These objects serve as external and physical symbolic manifestations of a teacher's professionalism, skill, education, and performance experience. Studio spaces were also highly divergent in presentation, from a stylishly clean, almost clinical teaching space with ordered folders and designated "student space" and "teacher space", to spaces with lounges, scarves, bits of props from productions, music folders stacked up high on the desk, and lamps creating a laid-back, cosy atmosphere. The way studio spaces worked were highly personal to the teacher. Notably, while in Australia it is common to see glass panels in the doors of teaching and practice rooms for transparency and safety purposes, this was not the case in any of the studios I visited in the United States. These spaces are private, where what happens "behind closed doors"[5] continues to lend a mystique to the practices of the singing voice teacher.

Signature pedagogies: Mapping the content, organisation, and approach to one-to-one singing pedagogy

Idiosyncratic approach to teaching

Mapping the content and structure of lessons during data analysis generated specific themes related to surface, implicit, and deep structures of one-to-one singing voice pedagogy in musical theatre programmes. Considering the surface structures of lessons, in terms of content there was only one commonality among all participants. Unsurprisingly, that common feature was teaching musical theatre repertoire. Apart from the performance of musical theatre repertoire, singing teachers approached the content and structure of lessons in idiosyncratic ways. The nature of the lessons as idiosyncratic became the first identifiable signature to one-to-one singing pedagogy. As an example of this idiosyncratic approach, one participant focused almost entirely on functional and technical work over the entire two weeks of observed lessons. In each lesson with this participant, repertoire was only used to enhance functional training. Students rarely sang through a verse of a song in its entirety without stopping for technical adjustment. Another teacher focused on repertoire performance skills and acting through the song, only very occasionally asking for technical adjustments (using critique[6]) during a lesson. Differences in teaching approaches *might* be attributed to the standard and development of the student in question. However, in both cases teachers used their pedagogical approach across all students in all years.[7] The teachers' individual, idiosyncratic preferences to the content and structure of lessons appeared to be the defining feature of the pedagogy.

When analysing lesson content, I noted that only four teachers spent time on bodywork and stretching within the lessons. This was interesting because unlike other musical instruments, the singing instrument is housed inside a human body and subject to the day-to-day tensions of the performer. The physiological condition of the singer can impact greatly on the way a singer is able to operate their voice. Of the teachers who used physical stretches, one teacher used the same series of stretches in every lesson with every student. Another used a variety of yoga positions to facilitate connection to body and breath flow. These teachers allocated specific time within the warm-up time of their lessons to do this work. Another teacher guided students in self massage using both external massage and tools such as an electronic massage gun and trigger point massage cane. The fourth teacher who regularly included bodywork was certified in a specific training modality which used a hands-on approach with students in every lesson. In this teacher's studio often half of the lesson time (and sometimes more) was spent on bodywork prior to moving into singing. Again, speaking to the idiosyncratic nature of one-to-one singing teaching, this participant spent considerably more time on bodywork and significantly less time on singing during lesson time when compared with other participants in this research.

While I suspect all teachers would declare that their teaching approach was "student-centred", this similar approach to teaching throughout their cohort of students often went unquestioned (and unnoticed?) by the participants. For example, those teachers who used bodywork, stretching, and body-breath connection seemed to assume that this was a standard way of teaching, just as those teachers who conducted no stretching, bodywork, or alignment and did not appear to consider that there was anything missing from their teaching. My comments here are in no way a criticism of the participant teachers and their work—I was careful in my observations to simply note what was being done in the moment.[8] This aspect of teacher preferences and routines regarding the content and structure of their lessons might speak to the isolation of singing lessons, and the fact that lessons are often conducted within a private space, often without any kind of peer review of the conduct of lessons. It is also possible that teachers were teaching lessons in ways they had observed, or experienced themselves, or in reaction to the way they themselves were taught to sing.

Repertoire considerations for musical theatre performers

When it came to musical theatre repertoire, a significant finding was that over the 193 lessons across the 6 different sites only twice did I observe repeated repertoire selections. While the signature pedagogies of private music lessons have previously been described as using "the standard repertoire of the individual instrument",[9] in musical theatre lessons there appeared to be no "standard" repertoire. Indeed, it was notable that over the course of 12 weeks I rarely heard repertoire from any of the most popular, well known musical theatre productions. Not once did I hear a song from *Cats, Les Miserables, Hamilton, Phantom of the Opera, A Chorus Line, Chicago, Cabaret, The Lion King*, or other long running, highly visible musical theatre productions. This diversity of repertoire is a signature of the content of musical theatre singing lessons, and the requirement for the voice teacher to know and have access to a wide range of repertoire is an *implicit* structure of musical theatre voice pedagogy. Students performed a variety of different musical theatre styles within this diverse repertoire including belt, mix, and legit songs from different time periods within the scope of musical theatre history.

Classical voice training in the musical theatre programme

A common term used by those teaching music theatre *and* classical genres is *cross training*.[10] This term is generally used to describe how classical singers learn the necessary vocal function and stylistic changes required to sing the traditional music theatre styles of belt, legit, or mix.[11] However, there is also literature supporting cross training to classical singing for musical theatre artists.[12] The concept of cross training appears to have emerged from classically trained pedagogues assisting students to find increased performance opportunities within musical theatre. It has also become a standard term in classical voice literature for pragmatic reasons, as increasing numbers of students wish to learn genres other than classical.[13] However, traditional legit singing style, which is more closely associated with the classical genre, is less common than in the past, and legit singing has changed to a new contemporary style which is strongly influenced by rock and pop.[14] In musical theatre training, cross training requires students to be able to sing classical style and function, as well as the ability to sing in appropriate style and function for contemporary music theatre, including belt and mix singing.

At four of the six universities visited, classical voice selections were included in student training and placed in their musical theatre audition book as a demonstration of singing skill. In one case the teacher commented that students are "not expected to be a classical singer—this [learning a classical piece in a foreign language] is just to expose him to opera quality and foreign language singing".[15] At another university a teacher specifically told me that classical voice was included in the curriculum for academic purposes, teaching students how to engage with unfamiliar material. Other universities with classical repertoire included in the musical theatre programme appeared to have the repertoire there by default, rather than for specific industry or academic relevance for musical theatre training.

Notably, at one university students had lessons with classical voice teachers for the first year and a half of their programme. After this period students could audition to become a musical theatre major. Upon acceptance to the musical theatre major the students switched to musical theatre specialist teachers. The musical theatre teachers noted that they often had to retrain the voices, spending at least half a year removing classical technique from students' voices, so students could sing the musical theatre repertoire with appropriate style and functionality.

That it was considered acceptable for students intending to major in musical theatre to learn classical singing for a year and a half is an example of the "tension surrounding professional preparation, from the competing demands of academy and profession".[16] The concept that classical voice training and repertoire is the appropriate foundation for contemporary musical theatre singing was directly problematic for teachers in this institution. Recalling that AATS declared that a classical voice technique "does not automatically nor easily reconfigure to produce sounds that are typical stylistic requirements of CCM repertoire",[17] it is notable that these students receive a year and a half less training in their specific chosen singing style compared to students in other musical theatre programmes. By contrast, the opposite situation is almost unthinkable. It is hard to imagine classical voice teachers being asked to allow classical voice students to have only CCM or musical theatre specialist teachers teaching them for the first year and a half of a classical performance degree. Yet musical theatre teachers are expected to accept this situation, despite it conceivably placing their students behind other graduates in terms of vocal development upon entry into a highly competitive workforce.

Furthermore, while learning classical style and function,[18] foreign language skills are required. While this is undoubtedly a useful academic exercise in learning unfamiliar material, the time within a degree is limited. Can time spent on classical voice training and the attendant language skills be warranted within a musical theatre degree? Riffing, improvisation, stylistic nuances, and functional, technical skills are essential CCM additions to a musical theatre voice teacher's toolbox. Consideration must be given to how long it might take students to learn the stylistic nuances and skills appearing within contemporary musical theatre repertoire. Only one participant teacher did *not* require musical theatre students to perform classical repertoire. Notably this teacher had a specific and structured four-year curriculum designed specifically to address the many different CCM styles and their attendant voice functions that students may require during their musical theatre career.

CCM training in the musical theatre programme

The initial focus of the study was to examine how teachers prepared students for the many CCM styles now present in contemporary musical theatre productions. During my time observing lessons, CCM style, function and repertoire were taught in two main ways: through specific technical exercises and through repertoire.

CCM technique training

In terms of CCM technical requirements, while a few teachers used specific technical training for CCM singing (including registrational focus on chest- dominant sound in females, speech-style articulation, airflow, and a variety of onset and offset choices), I observed only one example of a teacher adjusting a scale to train a riff (a common stylistic event in CCM) over the 193 lessons observed. Analysis of the data further exposed that exercises were mostly sung in major keys. Rhythm was rarely addressed in the technical work using any kind of CCM-specific approach other than a standard straight 4/4 beat, or occasionally a swung tempo, although teachers did specifically address rhythmic issues when working on CCM repertoire. When teachers addressed CCM function in the lesson, they generally used two distinct approaches—either as a way for students to compare different ways of singing functionally to adjust between genres (this was rare), or in direct response to student rehearsal, audition, and repertoire needs (more common). While a few teachers did address specific CCM function and style, this was by no means usual, and, by comparison, nearly all teachers explicitly addressed the technical and stylistic differences between classical voice technique and musical theatre singing.

The lack of specific function and style training in CCM genres such as pop, rock, country, and R&B would perhaps be expected in a musical theatre programme were it not for the prevalence of these CCM genres in contemporary musical theatre productions. Only two participant teachers worked specifically on CCM function and styles consistently with students. However, most one-to-one lessons had minimal inclusion of any kind of specific stylistic traits of singing aside from those relevant to musical theatre and classical voice training. I found it strange to consider the amount of time spent comparing classical functionality with musical theatre functionality in lessons, especially when I considered that students were far more likely to be employed in musical theatre where they would need to sing pop, rock, country, hip hop, rather than opera or classical singing. Considering classical students undertake four-year degrees, plus years of private lessons and coaching, and often master's and doctoral degrees to perform classical styles expertly, one would assume that these performers would be employed to sing classical repertoire over musical theatre performers in a typical audition situation.

CCM singing was also addressed in group classes. At one university, CCM was addressed through a group pedagogy class where students learnt the specific functional and stylistic differences between CCM and musical theatre genres. At two universities CCM was addressed in group classes for the musical theatre students, specifically working through different CCM genres and stylistic choices within the genres. These classes progressed through different time periods each week, from the 1950s to the present day, examining CCM genres through a sociological lens, examining the different types of CCM genres found within the time period. The teachers involved in these programmes were clear that musical theatre students would be required to sing in CCM styles in their career and focused on providing a framework for students to be able to adapt their singing voices to sing CCM repertoire.

CCM repertoire training

The inclusion of CCM repertoire in the one-to-one studios of the teachers I observed followed two patterns. CCM repertoire was either specifically included in the structure of the syllabus, or brought into the class by the student for performance or audition practice. Students at four programmes were working within the first structure and expected to have genre specific CCM songs in their jury repertoire, and this expectation was built into the syllabus. Two programmes had a more oblique approach to CCM genres in musical theatre. In these programmes students brought

CCM repertoire to lessons and the teachers worked with them. Students were observed to be expected to be able to adjust to these styles on their own—functional and stylistic differences were not addressed in a specific way by teachers. However, I did observe other teachers adjust their pedagogical approaches to address the issues within lessons when working with CCM material. This occurred in two different ways.

The first manner of CCM-focused adjustments were very slight and non-specific. In this case, students were left to interpret what was expected of them functionally and stylistically. The second type of adjustment involved confident, highly directive instruction, guiding the student to engage with the genres in question in a specific way. The teachers who used specific direction when working with CCM songs had attended professional development via branded voice teaching methods specifically focused on CCM voice pedagogy. In each case this professional development occurred after the completion of their own university training.

Interestingly, four of the six universities I visited were in rehearsal with CCM musicals during my visit. These productions included a variety of CCM genres—rock, country, gospel, pop, folk, and 1950s rock 'n' roll. One university was producing a legit-style musical and another a Disney "movical". However, few students brought functional and stylistic issues from these CCM productions to lessons. Those that did bring material to lessons were focused on solving problems connected to the physicality of being a musical theatre performer, for example, where specific choreography or blocking had impacted on their vocal performance. I observed students bring specific stylistic issues from their rehearsals into the studio room in only 2 lessons out of the 193 observed.

During the lesson times I observed students prepare repertoire for other kinds of specific performances, such as showcases and cabarets. This material appeared to be more explicitly connected to voice development, as opposed to performances in productions which may be graded differently. These grading considerations might include a student's acting skills, or the developmental synergy of triple threat skills, for example, rather than only vocal performance and development. The accrediting bodies for music and theatre in higher education, the National Association of Schools of Music (NASM) and the National Association of Schools of

Theatre (NAST) provide guidelines students in undergraduate programmes must have

> Opportunities for performances in workshop and full productions of musical theatre in a variety of formal and informal settings. Performance of a significant role in at least one full production during advanced study is regarded as an essential experience.[19]

In addition, the NASM states that "at all times, the choice and preparation of performance must be directly related to the education of singer-actors or actor-singers ... Levels of vocal maturity must be carefully considered in the choice of repertory".[20] While the question of voice teacher consultation on production choices and casting in terms of student voice development was outside of the scope of this study, indications that discussion between those in positions of authority to cast productions and voice teachers at some schools appeared minimal—this may be an area where further research is required.

One teacher specifically addressed this in a discussion with me, commenting that students in classical programmes were expected to perform pieces which were developmentally appropriate within their four year or graduate programmes, whereas musical theatre students were expected to perform the roles they were cast in, regardless of whether teachers felt they could comfortably perform those roles at that stage in their vocal development. This was demonstrated dramatically in a lesson where a freshman student was preparing an audition callback for a student production. After the lesson the teacher commented that the student might be cast because "they looked great for the role" but that they were concerned that the student was not vocally ready for performance of the singing requirements of the character.

To conclude, in terms of CCM styles and musical theatre programmes, only one programme did **not** have student performances of CCM repertoire built into the performance expectations of students, although I observed students prepare CCM songs in their lessons at this site. In fact, at every university site I visited I observed students bring CCM-style repertoire to the private voice class. The CCM genres being performed in the lessons I observed included country, pop, rock, R&B, and gospel. Despite the proliferation of CCM singing in musical theatre programmes, teachers had diverse approaches to specificity when addressing CCM repertoire, from ignoring stylistic and functional issues in the repertoire to giving specific and direct advice on appropriate vocalisation. Confidence and specificity when addressing CCM styles was directly related to how much training a teacher had received in both singing and the pedagogy of CCM singing styles. In all cases, this training in CCM pedagogy and practice was conducted outside of the teacher's training in higher education.

What was missing from lessons?

Amplification training

One element of voice training missing from the musical theatre voice studios was teaching students to how to work with microphones. Musical theatre productions use body worn microphones, and some productions rely on handheld microphones (e.g., *Six*). Musical theatre performers need to understand how to use microphones, and the impact that microphones have on the voice, particularly in cabaret-style performances. One of the characteristics of CCM singing is that it is amplified and mixed through a mixing desk. A sound engineer can boost or reduce various frequencies in a singer's voice to assist with the way the voice is perceived in the theatre, as well as add in many effects. The use of microphones allows for a sound engineer to equalize, or EQ the voice in relation to the other instrumentation. Equalisation of the voice may alter the natural acoustic principles of the voice which may be helpful if a singer is unwell.[21] This is important information for performers which can ensure they do not over-sing, which may cause vocal problems in future performances.

Four studios had small portable sound systems which teachers could use with students; however, I didn't see any teachers use these systems during my observations, even when students were performing CCM styles. In an audition a performer needs to understand the acoustic of the room and how it might influence their ability to perform in that space, and auditions are not amplified, so understanding how to use the voice in an audition room compared to when performing with a band in a CCM environment outside of musical theatre might explain this discrepancy.

However, performers still need to understand how body-worn mics can assist them to avoid voice overuse—this microphone is an extension of every contemporary musical theatre performer. Aspiring performers might need to be trained in how these microphones work, and how good microphone technique can assist them in terms of reducing vocal load during long contracts. The sensitivity of microphones can be exploited for expressive purposes by performers and while this training may happen with sound technicians from a university, rather than studio voice teachers, this issue was not addressed nor discussed in any studio I observed.

Additionally, while teachers may want amplification resources for their students, the teaching environment may not make this possible. A teacher commented that they already had soundproofing issues with her neighbouring faculty member, and so a sound system, while desirable, would be detrimental to her relationship with that staff member. At another university, there was a lack of amplification not only in the teaching studio, but into the performance space. For example:

> University Q has no microphones for students to work with, and no sound systems for them to work on and learn understand how using a microphone affects their sound choices. HQ, and other students, are doing lots of pop-rock styles in their senior seminar, which they know how to do with stylistic authenticity, but because they are performing this in a theatre (rather than a small audition room, where their voices would carry well), they are having to change how they sing these songs to project them, rather than sing them in the appropriate and authentic CCM style.[22]

A lack of access to amplification did not set the students up appropriately for the contemporary musical theatre environment or teach them how to sing with appropriate style. At this site teachers understood the role of amplification. However, they were repeatedly undermined by another faculty member who used their power within the department hierarchy to refuse their calls for amplification to be provided to students when performing in the large auditorium space. The faculty member who blocked the use of amplification was a member of the costume department and did not understand the requirements of vocal production or vocal health.

Dance

Synthesis of the skills of acting, dance, and singing is essential to the musical theatre performer. Synthesis of dance and singing was an approach used by only two teachers in the musical theatre studios I observed. In one studio there was a directly oppositional approach to dance and singing as the teacher worked with the student to *release* the tension the student embodied through their dance class, while another teacher actively encouraged the student to *engage* with dancing and singing at the same time. The training of musical theatre performers needs to tailored to their specific needs, and teachers ideally understand "the biomechanical imperatives associated with acting, singing, and dancing simultaneously".[23] Commenting on the use of breath for singing for musical theatre performers who must sing and dance at the same time, Wilson warns: "the singing teacher that advises a singer/dancer/actor to 'Just release all those tight belly muscles' in order to facilitate breath support, is inviting disaster of one kind or another".[24]

While there has been research on the different breathing approaches of different body types,[25] the limited research which has been produced on dancing, singing, and breath support suggests that one skill is compromised for the other when dancing and singing are combined.[26] There is little guidance in the literature for working with singer/actors about how to provide a clear pathway to achieving singing optimal results when dancing. This lack of research into the singer/dancer/actor may explain why few teachers addressed this issue in the studio practices observed for this study. Through interviews and reports on collaborative approaches in productions, Melton[27] presents a different viewpoint. Discussing an experience working with students in a production of *Cats*, she comments that it is possible for performers to synthesise dancing, acting, and singing using the Laban approach, efficiency of breath management, a focus on text phrasing, and integration of voice and movement elements during rehearsal period. There have been recent calls for increased collaborative approaches between dance and voice teachers within musical theatre programmes to assist students to synthesise these skills.[28] The pedagogy assisting students in the synthesis of dance and singing skills is an area requiring further research.

Why are lessons so idiosyncratic?

As stated earlier, the pedagogical approach of musical theatre voice teachers was highly idiosyncratic. Teachers might warm up their students and spend time on technical work, or they might not. They may work on CCM repertoire in specific detail, or merely listen to it. Teachers might devote time to teaching students classical style, repertoire, and function, or they might ignore this genre of music altogether. All teachers taught musical theatre styles and repertoire, addressing speech quality, legit, belt, and mix singing. Some teachers, in addition to the above considerations, addressed acting through singing and assisted students to develop acting choices within their lesson.

This view into the private world of the singing lesson revealed the idiosyncrasy of the profession, as well as some revealing exclusions. Why did some teachers insist on the inclusion of Western classical repertoire, spending time on the foreign language requirements and stylistic and functional intricacies of this music, while others completely ignored this element of lessons? Why did some teachers address specific functional and stylistic nuances of different CCM styles in detail, while others merely nodded and moved onto something else in the lesson? What did teachers themselves consider important in their teaching approaches, and why? And why were some elements of singing CCM (such as engagement with a microphone and the impact of the microphone on singing) completely absent within lessons? Underpinning these questions was a larger question: How did teachers learn to teach singing?

Notes

1 Don et al., 2009.
2 Ibid., p. 90.
3 Shulman, 2005, p. 54.
4 Boardman, 1987.
5 Carey & Grant, 2015, p. 6.
6 See Don et al. (2009).

7 Further, a teacher *might* teach students function at one time in a semester and repertoire coaching towards the end of a semester in preparation for performance exams, or "juries". As I visited universities in two-week blocks over the academic year, this may be a limitation to the study.
8 It became clear to me, as a fellow teacher, that all of these approaches appeared to be of utility to students. However, I had decided not to try and "judge effectiveness" in my study because effectiveness in singing teaching is measured in diverse ways (student success, student employment upon graduation). Based on the notion of motor learning, skill acquisition is usually built gradually over time rather than over one or two lesson. Indeed, my subjectivity as a professional voice teacher and performer was acknowledged throughout by the use of a reflexive journal where I noted my biases and own teaching preferences. It was helpful in spending time observing teachers over more than a few lessons in order to understand their approaches and to notice what teachers did which was similar or different to my own practices. In fact, I noted that this observational work overcame some of my noted prejudices against certain approaches to teaching singing. Further, this process shed light on my own strengths and shortcomings within my own teaching practice. Again, I am grateful for the generosity of my participant teachers who allowed me access to their teaching.
9 Don et al., 2009, p. 90.
10 Spivey & Saunders-Barton, 2018.
11 Bos, 2010; Browning, 2016; Catania, 2004; Cooper, 2003; Ness, 2014; Spivey & Saunders-Barton, 2018.
12 Browning, 2016; Edwin, 2008; Spivey & Saunders-Barton, 2018; Turnbow et al., 2014.
13 Catania, 2004.
14 Edwin, 2003.
15 Interview transcription, AQ.
16 Shulman, 2005, p. 53.
17 American Academy of Teachers of Singing, 2008.
18 Cross training function and styles associated with classical singing may have skill acquisition value particularly in consideration of legit singing and when considering elite musical theatre belting. LeBorgne (2001) discusses the presence of skilled vibrato and ring in elite belters, and these skills are traditionally associated with classical training. However, the participant teachers themselves did not discuss specifically the importance of teaching vibrato or ring in relation to teaching CCM or musical theatre, and I did not observe specific training of ring or vibrato, even when teachers were teaching classical repertoire and function.

19 NASM, 2020, p. 116; NAST, 2019, p. 97.
20 NASM, 2020, p. 162; NAST, 2019, p. 141.
21 The sound engineer for Hamilton explains this in this video: www.youtube.com/watch?v=60OpF3DCVls from 2 minutes 20 seconds.
22 Reflexive notes, University Q.
23 Wilson, 2010, p. 297.
24 Ibid.
25 Griffith Cowgill, 2009.
26 Sliiden et al., 2016.
27 Melton, 2015.
28 Kvammen et al., 2020.

References

American Academy of Teachers of Singing. (2008). *In Support of Contemporary Commercial Music (nonclassical) voice pedagogy*. www.americanacademyofteachersofsinging.org/assets/articles/CCMVoicePedagogy.pdf

Boardman, S. (1987). *Voice training for the musical theatre singer*. (Doctor of Musical Arts in Voice). Retrieved from ProQuest database. (8722053)

Bos, N. (2010). The courage for change. *Journal of Singing, 66*(3), 315–317.

Browning, R. (2016). Crossover concerns and techniques for the classical singer. *Journal of Singing, 72*(5), 609–617.

Carey, G., & Grant, C. (2015). Teacher and student perspectives on one-to-one pedagogy: Practices and possibilities. *British Journal of Music Education, 32*(1), 5–22. doi: 10.1017/S0265051714000084

Catania, C. (2004). Music theatre as a technical tool and pragmatic business choice for the classical singer. *Journal of Singing, 61*(2), 185–186.

Cooper, G. (2003). Once more with feeling: The crossover artist's first steps in making an emotional connection with a popular or jazz song. *Journal of Singing, 60*(2), 153–157.

Don, G., Garvey, C., & Sedeghpour, M. (2009). Theory and practice: Signature pedagogies in music theory and performance. In R. Gurung, N. Chick & A. Haynie (Eds.), *Exploring more signature pedagogies* (pp. 81–98). Stylus.

Edwin, R. (2003). A broader Broadway. *Journal of Singing, 59*(5), 431–432.

Edwin, R. (2008). Cross training for the voice. *Journal of Singing, 65*(1), 73–76.

Griffith Cowgill, J. (2009). Breathing for singers: A comparative analysis of body types and breathing tendencies. *Journal of Singing, 66*(2), 141–147.

Kvammen, A. C., Hagen, J. K., & Parker, S. (2020). Exploring new methodical options: Collaborative teaching involving song, dance and the Alexander Technique. *International Journal of Education & the Arts, 21*(7). doi: 10.26209/ijea21n7/

LeBorgne, W. (2001). Defining the belt voice: Perceptual judgements and objective measures. (UMI 3028707). [Doctoral dissertation, University of Cincinnati]. Proquest.

Melton, J. (2015). *Dancing with voice: A collaborative journey across disciplines.* CreateSpace Independent Publishing Platform.

National Association of Schools of Music (January 21, 2020). *National Association of Schools of Music handbook.* https://nasm.arts-accredit.org/wp-content/uploads/sites/2/2020/01/M-2019-20-Handbook-02-13-2020.pdf

National Association of Schools of Theatre, (April 19, 2019). *National Association of Schools of Theatre handbook.* https://nast.arts-accredit.org/wp-content/uploads/sites/4/2019/05/NAST-Handbook-2019-20-Current-08-30-2019.pdf

Ness, C. (2014). Teaching music theatre: An integrative dialectical approach. *The Opera Journal, 47*(1), 3–32.

Shulman, L. (2005). Signature pedagogies in the professions. *Daedalus, 134*(3), 52–59.

Sliiden, T., Beck, S., & MacDonald, I. (2016). An evaluation of the breathing strategies and maximum phonation time in musical theater performers during controlled performance tasks. *Journal of Voice, 31*(2), 253.e.1–253.e.11.

Spivey, N., & Saunders-Barton, M. (2018). *Cross-training in the voice studio: A balancing act.* Plural.

Turnbow, C., Saunders-Barton, M., & Spivey, N. (2014). Training the next generation of music theater voice teachers: Penn State's first MFA pedagogy grad takes stock. *Journal of Singing, 71*(2), 217–220.

Wilson, P. (2010). Showtime!—Teaching musical theatre and cabaret singing. In S. Harrison (Eds.), *Perspectives on teaching singing: Australian vocal pedagogues sing their stories* (pp. 293–305). Australian Academic Press.

4 Where did you learn to teach?

Training backgrounds of musical theatre singing teachers

It is not unusual for musical theatre students to be taught singing by teachers who experienced considerable training in the classical music tradition. Each of the voice teachers I interviewed, and a majority of those observed, had both undergraduate and graduate degrees in classical voice performance. Musical theatre students in higher education continue to be taught by not only by teachers whose specialty and training is classical voice training, but who often have little to no pedagogical training in contemporary singing styles. An example of this was unequivocally demonstrated at one university, where there was only one musical theatre voice specialist on faculty (who had a classical voice performance training background, but experience performing in musical theatre). This teacher was engaged to train the musical theatre singers for only one year of their degree, with the remaining three years of private voice lessons in the degree allocated to classical voice faculty. The classical faculty who trained the students for the remaining years of their degrees had demonstrated experience and skill at teaching and maintained impressive CVs both in performance and pedagogy. However, it remained that it was through backgrounds in classical voice performance and training that these faculty members promoted and practiced their teaching. Additionally, according to the university website where biographies of voice teaching faculty were available, only *one* of the classical voice faculty members had any experience in performing in legit-style musical theatre. While this specific university provides a notable

DOI: 10.4324/9781003332572-4

example of this phenomenon, the situation at this site was not unique. Several participating institutions used classical voice faculty, who possessed little to no experience or education in musical theatre voice pedagogy, to train musical theatre students to sing.

Research participants were candid about their lack of musical theatre voice training, particularly in their own academic education. One teacher had undergraduate, master's, and doctoral qualifications in classical vocal performance. It was only during this participant's doctoral programme that they experienced a voice teacher who assisted her to access her chest register (essential for musical theatre and CCM singing for females). This experience occurred at the age of 24, after many years of voice lessons. She then moved interstate, opened a private studio, and worked with teenagers who needed to belt to sing musical theatre. She began to train with another teacher who worked in CCM genres at a nearby university, as well as a "master teacher" from a specific private pedagogical method, to understand how to train her teenage students in musical theatre style and function. She describes her post academic training experiences and how her own voice responded:

> Um, so, at the very beginning it was probably more pseudo belting. More head dominance, you know ... and, and gradually as I acquired more skills through, you know, going to conferences and training and things like that I was able to, um, to I think get closer to an industry sound.[1]

When I asked the participant about the percentage of lessons taken in classical voice compared to CCM (including musical theatre) genres, she responded: "Oh, my God, whoo. Really, 98% classical, 2% CCM".[2] The 2% of post-doctoral retraining has been invaluable to the participant's teaching career as she teaches musical theatre and CCM singing genres in her university position. This teacher trained no classical voice students in her position, despite classical singing forming the entire basis for her academic training.

Another participant had undergraduate and master's degrees in acting and classical voice performance, was pursuing doctoral studies in classical voice performance but left graduate school to work in New York:

I trained myself, honestly, it kind of worked ... I kept going into auditions and half the time they would say "you're singing too much" and I had no idea what that meant. ... in vocal departments, or in musical theatre departments they would study with classical voice teachers primarily, which was often in opposition to what they were actually doing.[3]

With a similar background story, another teacher held undergraduate and master's degrees in classical voice performance and commented on the historic lack of musical theatre-specific voice teaching available in HME. This participant worked with a private vocal coach after graduation to access appropriate training. It was this additional training which led to the understanding of musical theatre voice pedagogy and practices.[4]

Participant AQ gained an undergraduate degree in music education followed by a graduate performance degree in classical voice, and then proceeded to have a successful professional musical theatre performance career. AQ felt that classical voice training did not provide enough pedagogical information for them to teach musical theatre voice styles and invested in further CCM voice pedagogy training to further develop appropriate pedagogical skills. This training was undertaken *after* years of employment teaching music theatre students at the university level. Classical qualifications combined with musical theatre performance experience (as well as considerable musicianship skills) were considered an appropriate background for employment as a university musical theatre voice teacher.

Participant AT was trained in musical theatre singing styles (belt and legit) by private teachers outside of the university system. This teacher's skill at being able to cross over between musical theatre and classical was a factor for AT in gaining entrance to a master's programme; however once enrolled AT discovered the musical theatre specialist teacher who recruited them was not their private voice teacher. AT was not encouraged to perform musical theatre repertoire and musical theatre-specific function was not addressed during academic training:

> AT: So, for me, when I learned how to belt, that totally opened my whole voice up, I actually had substance in the sound and she [the graduate studies voice teacher] almost took all that away. And she really, she was very much like "NO! you will not

sing like that." So, as much as I tried to fight it, she was constantly on me and everyone else there sang in this very sort of off the voice in a light way. ... The reason I took a year off after masters was to rebuild again. I went back and worked with (the private teachers) again during that year. To rebuild my instrument, *again*.[5]

What was particularly frustrating to this participant was that they had been accepted to the master's programme based on their ability to sing in musical theatre style, and was told that they would get further training with a musical theatre specialist teacher, yet in practice was actively discouraged from progressing in those skills during their studies.

Interestingly, while three participants held undergraduate musical theatre degrees, one of these teachers was taught mostly classical voice function and style by her undergraduate musical theatre voice teacher. This participant went on to do a graduate degree in classical performance, and it was in voice lessons with me (requested as part of the principle of reciprocity and using participant observation during the site visit) that the teacher discovered firstly what chest register felt like in her own voice, and secondly, how to belt. Considering the teacher was already employed to teach singing in a musical theatre voice programme, belt is one of the defining features of musical theatre voice singing, and this teacher had an undergraduate degree in musical theatre, the question of a how a female performer graduates from a musical theatre degree without the ability to sing in a functional belt is relevant.

This example further signifies the importance of specific stylistic and functional training of music theatre voice students not only for employability, but because performance students often become teachers. Graduate employment outcomes in the performing arts is a topic of research in the United Kingdom and Australia[6] where teaching is understood to be a common career trajectory for performing arts graduates.[7] Additionally, appropriate teacher training for those *teaching* musical theatre students would seem to be a basic and obvious requirement of employment within a university setting where expertise is highly prized by both the institution and students alike.

Participants discussed openly, and were sensitive to gaps in their teaching skills and actively looked for training opportunities.

One participant was interested in finding a doctoral programme to improve her skillset. The difficulty of finding a suitable programme in the United States meant attending short (2–9 days) voice teaching method courses available during the summer break to gain these skills. This teacher was acutely aware of the career limitations placed on them in their employment by not having a doctorate. Frustratingly they were unable to financially afford to take the time off work to complete this qualification and progress their career. Accessibility is a huge consideration for those teachers and performers already working, who would like the opportunity to study CCM pedagogy more intensely. The two main barriers were the lack of graduate-level CCM programmes available, and the lack of online doctoral programmes focusing on CCM-specific voice pedagogy. Many universities in the United States continue to require graduate students to leave their established workplaces, existing family support structures, and communities, to gain doctoral degrees. It should be noted that permanent positions often require a terminal degree. In the field of voice pedagogy this is a doctorate, not a master's, and as I noted, there are few doctoral degrees which specialise in either musical theatre or contemporary singing pedagogy.

What were teachers' experiences as students?

I asked participants during interviews if they had access to learning musical theatre singing styles during their academic training. Nearly all participants who had experienced an exclusively classical voice training responded that they were not given any opportunity to try to sing musical theatre styles during their university education. Participants commented that singing a belted sound was particularly taboo. These teachers, when students, were occasionally allowed to sing legit-style musical theatre repertoire using their classical technique. The fact that teachers direct what students are *allowed* to perform indicates the degree of power some singing teachers can hold over students. One participant commented that some classical teachers actively discouraged the performance of musical theatre singing styles:

> I remember I auditioned at University I for my masters, and the teacher I had a sample lesson, she was like "you can't do that

musical theatre", she said. She was like "If you're going to do opera, you're a dramatic soprano. You **have** to focus on this." And she was like "Why would you even do that [musical theatre repertoire]?" I mean, a lot of people ... [said] it was going to hurt me or that it just was asking something *so* completely different of my instrument that if I had any serious chances of a performance career in opera, I shouldn't waste my time.[8]

Note that in this example the teachers who AT auditioned for who actively dissuaded them from performing musical theatre styles *acknowledged* that classical technique would not serve musical theatre singing. Other participants noted that there was no discussion about the academic instruction of musical theatre because it was simply absent from their university music training experience: "There was no other training to be had".[9]

Participants also commented on the lack of general pedagogical training in their performance degrees. If a teacher did receive pedagogical training, it was usually in relation to classical voice technique. Only one participant out of thirteen had a graduate degree which was specific to musical theatre voice pedagogy, and one had a voice science-based qualification. Three of the participant teachers had experienced a pedagogy class as a part of their graduate training which focused on classical approaches to voice pedagogy. The remaining teachers had performance-based degrees with little to no pedagogical training other than observation of their own teachers. Interestingly this was the case with both older participants (nearing the end of their teaching careers) and younger participants (within five years of entering teaching in academia full time). While graduate degrees based on CCM and musical theatre voice pedagogy are emerging, they are still not necessarily as easy to access in higher education as a classically based voice degree.

Participants also discussed their own challenges as learners within the HME system. Their own experiences as students weighed on them in the way they approached their own teaching. One teacher described working during their academic training by performing musical theatre songs at night. They commented:

> musical theatre actually fit my voice significantly better than a classical track, that my voice always stuck in between, and they

[my teachers] would try to move me up to tenor, and it didn't really feel good, but yet I wasn't a baritone, and so musical theatre just fit.[10]

Despite musical theatre singing being a good fit, they experienced active discouragement from their singing teachers in the university setting: "he thought I would never make a living as a singer. And that's crushing to a 22-year-old, right? **Crushing**".[11] Comments like this raise the ethical question of why a university would accept someone for a graduate degree in voice performance who the faculty felt would not be successful in a career, despite receiving the expert standard of training expected to be provided by higher education. Was this an acknowledgement that the teacher did not have the expertise to assist the student to learn the required skills to become a professional in the field?

The expertise of instructors has been found to be one of the most important pedagogical characteristics for learners in higher education settings.[12] The decisive and absoluteness of the negative comment experienced by this participant is an example of the power dynamic in the studio—this type of critique can have strong psychological impacts on students. While this student did have a successful performance career, despite this teacher's opinion and active discouragement, how many other students simply gave up? Further, the power dynamic in the one-to-one studio means that comments like these may go unchallenged by other, more informed, voices.

Perhaps because of the anonymity guaranteed to participants, teachers freely discussed the impact of their own experiences as learners and the impact of their past teachers on their pedagogical approach. Teachers who had experienced difficulties in their own educational experience, whether from a preference for CCM and musical theatre styles, or from a sense of being unsupported in their own artistic pursuits, described how they used these experiences in a foundational way to develop their own teaching philosophy. The participant who was told they would not be a successful singer commented: "I vowed that I would never do that as a teacher. My job is to make them sing **better**. Not necessarily to be a predictor of what their career is …"[13] This philosophy was reflected in my own observational notes where I noted this teacher's approach to pedagogy. The teacher often clearly articulated the concept of the

Where did you learn to teach? 57

student as a developing performance artist during lessons while addressing the development of technical skill. During discussions this participant described working closely with colleagues to develop an appropriate pedagogical approach to teaching musical theatre vocal techniques to students. Nevertheless, it was the concept of student as a developing artist which was the foundational philosophy upon which technique was structured and deployed within the participant's lessons. This is a clear example of the way teacher experiences in their own learning situation can impact on their later teaching practices.

Where did *teachers learn musical theatre and CCM singing?*

Participants expressed the need to go *outside* of their academic experiences in classical voice performance training to gain competence and confidence in their teaching roles. Universities and conservatories might demand classical performance degrees at the master's or doctoral level to gain access to university employment in the field of musical theatre voice teaching, but the degrees higher education produces did not meet the demands of teaching singing genres which were *not* classical in function or style. Participants described confronting the difficulty of completing an undergraduate, master's, and (in some cases) doctoral degree only to be unable to get performance work in musical theatre. To add insult to injury, they found that their degrees, which assisted them to get employment teaching the musical theatre styles now demanded by their employers, did not adequately prepare them for their work as teachers of musical theatre singing styles. This meant they required additional training both in pedagogy and practice to be able to teach this singing style with authenticity and confidence.

Participating musical theatre singing teachers agreed that there are functional and stylistic differences between classical and musical theatre or CCM singing styles. Embodying classical singing styles was not useful to participants when training musical theatre students. Teachers discussed the need to understand *and* embody the differences between classical and more contemporary singing styles in their own voices to be able to both sing and teach musical theatre. The ability to embody this practice in their own voices was perceived as central to their competence and confidence to teach musical theatre singing. Participants discussed being proactive about addressing their own lack of specific training by seeking further instruction. This instruction came from three main sources. Firstly, teachers paid for private lessons with more experienced musical theatre voice teachers or coaches. Secondly, participants discussed working collaboratively with colleagues to work out the intricacies of the differences between musical theatre singing and classical singing. The third approach was the active pursuit of organised professional development opportunities to acquire further training, often through short summer courses and conference and workshop attendance.

While all participants were confident discussing their transition from classical performer to musical theatre teacher, they often described being less confident in their abilities to transition into performing and teaching CCM styles such as rock, pop, R&B, country, and jazz. A younger teacher described their preparation for a concert where they would be singing "an opera aria, all the way through hip hop, R&B, and jazz".[14] This teacher described nervousness at approaching jazz singing:

> I really wanna do that because I feel like vocally I could do it, I just don't really understand it musically and stylistically. I understand it enough, I hear it, but I need to be, I need to have more training in that so, I'm reaching out for that.[15]

Teachers were aware of their own lack of training in different CCM styles and techniques, and some demonstrated their desire to be more specific with students through further training. Those teachers who had sought out CCM training were far more open to teaching with CCM-specific technique. I was interested to consider whether career stage played a role in openness to CCM-specific pedagogical training. One teacher, when asked about teaching rock, pop, and other CCM styles commented "I myself, could not one, demonstrate, not be able to demonstrate and two, would **never** be hired to sing that rep".[16] This teacher was about to retire from teaching and worked with students on their CCM repertoire to the best of their pedagogical ability. Another mature participant commented "… you know, popular music, so rock, or any other genre was never really my thing … I mean, I like it. I never really have the desire as much as musical theatre".[17]

Participant age, and years teaching, were not necessarily the defining factor of openness to CCM-specific training. One mature participant was excited about professional development courses and experiences working with various CCM-specific pedagogical teachers and spoke of the confidence gained from this process. A participant developed their personal CCM and musical theatre singing skills by taking three different branded voice teaching method training courses. Another younger teacher commented to me in a conversation that they felt uncomfortable pursuing this kind of training (via private instruction or one of the branded voice teaching methods) but was aware of the differences between CCM and musical theatre. However, when I asked them about professional development to learn CCM styles they responded:

AT: I would love to do that but I'm trying to get tenure so it's like, you only have so much money to do, so you might as well spend it going somewhere where you're gonna get a thing on your CV. Um, I'm trying to think if there's been one that I really wanted to audit. There's been a couple of things that, you know, I go to like The Voice Foundation or something that, you know, strikes a chord, or whatever. But a lot of the stuff just isn't very good.[18]

This teacher taught students CCM genres, knowing that it was important to help them become employable, and although they had never observed a CCM lesson, they had watched masterclasses, and online classes. AT commented further:

AT: Well, let me say this, and this may sound bad, but for a while there's no one doing CCM lessons here, so it's like, if I'm teaching it, and I feel like I'm a pretty good, like I can get the sound, I can get the sound, as far as voice technique, I'm not talking about stylistic things cause those I could definitely go to like, a jazz coach, and observe those, because that would help immensely! But vocal wise, not that I don't need to observe, it's just that I feel like it works.
R: Mm hmm
AT: And, who else am I going to observe? There might be, like, three people, maybe ... I just don't know of a

lot of people here. You know, operatic teaching, sure. I could, like, name a list. You know, of people to go observe.

R: So, most of the lessons you've observed, they've been classical?

AT: Most, yes.[19]

Teacher CV was comfortable in their expertise within musical theatre, had not trained in any specific CCM styles, and was able to bring outside teachers in to help with stylistic issues in CCM for students:

CV: Um, I've seen, I've been to workshops, I've been to, um, worked, had experts in my studio, had experts in come to school ... who really focus on that, and we will continue to do that. I don't know if my strength will ever be anything other than a dramatic form of music.[20]

Teacher AG was classically trained with no CCM training and used intuition, "expert ears", and pedagogical skills to help students adjust to appropriate CCM sounds. If this didn't work, AG sent send the students to another teacher on faculty who was more experienced in the area of CCM singing:

R: What about other contemporary styles like pop and rock? Have you had any sort of pedagogical training in those?

AG: Not exactly. Only because, oh case in point, only because if I just think about what I do.

R: Mm hmm

AG: I can kind of turn it into a more, for lack of a better word, cabaret sound, I can turn it more into "you have a microphone right in front of your face, so you're going to do it this way".

R: Mm hmm ...

R: So how do you help your students, because ... I've seen a few examples of when they come in and they have rock repertoire.

AG: Mm hmm

R: So, what's your approach to this repertoire?

AG:	Oh wow! I try to do a lot of listening to what is currently being hired.
R:	Mm hmm
AG:	Um, the sound that is now acceptable. Things like, um, XY's classes that I have gone to that I think he has a really great handle on how to get to that point.
R:	Mm hmm
AG:	So I guess I'm looking at placement, um,
R:	Which is a word you don't like to use!
AG:	I HATE that word. (laugh). But, let's say, well, we'll go back to my "point of departure", "where do you feel that sound leave a resonator?"
R:	Uh huh
AG:	And is the resonator actually just the microphone? Because all of those great things that XY does in those classes, I mean, let's just growl, OK, well, when he takes the mic away you don't hear anything!
R:	That's right!
AG:	Let's just see how much effort do you have to put into that?
R:	Yep
AG:	And then I send them to BG! (the pedagogy teacher on faculty).[21]

These teachers all articulated functional and stylistic differences between CCM genres and traditional musical theatre styles. However, it was clear that not all branded voice teaching methods address the differences between CCM styles in a specific and practical way:

R:	Have you had any specific sort of training in those or does (the branded voice teaching method this teacher used) approach those with specific, "OK, with these styles we do a specific sort of thing".
BX:	No, and in fact I'm not altogether sure that (the branded teaching method) ever gets, I mean, the model doesn't get there yet because, quite frankly, if you're thinking about the six archetype voice qualities that (the method), that we teach, CCM is not in there, really, you know.

R:	... Thanks. Um, so, you don't think (branded teaching method) ... addresses the particular CCM styles?
BX:	Not in so many words, I think only because, and this may be my own shortcoming about the application of these to CCM, this is where I look to my students to bring me the music and I apply what I know to them, but I hear certain things in some CCM music that's part of the style, um, maybe little bits of well-placed constriction, or some really power sounds that are not what we would call belt, and so I do what I can to help them. I can tell you, um, some of these people happen to be (proponents of the branded teaching method), which is fine, but the research they're doing may or may not be based on (the branded teaching method) work, it's an extension, there are a couple of people I know who are working very hard to do research on healthy growl, screech, I know that's not all there is,
R:	Mm hmm
BX:	to CCM, ... Other healthy ways to produce those because typically, probably not just the (branded teaching method) system, lots of systems, see those as potentially traumatic.
R:	Mm hmm
BX:	So, is there a way that we can teach them effectively and safely?
R:	Yup
BX:	And I'm all for that. It's, ah, it's not my wheelhouse necessarily, and that's when I see myself, OK, go somewhere and learn some of this stuff so I can bring it in.[22]

The deep structural assumption that classical voice training is appropriate to teaching musical theatre singers meant that teachers either learnt how to adjust their pedagogical skills using their own intuition and creativity, or where there was university support, took professional development courses to develop an ability to approach CCM styles. Teachers were acutely aware of their own training, of gaps in knowledge of style and function, and the need for further training to effectively teach CCM styles within their musical theatre programmes. However, they were not

Where did you learn to teach? 63

always clear on *where* to go to get appropriate training specific to CCM singing.

Why does specific training matter?

At best, students who graduate from musical theatre programmes with strong classical training but little experience or style-specific training in CCM genres might be considered under-educated and not adequately prepared for their desired career path. At worst they might experience vocal damage from attempting to perform CCM genres with classical function.[23] Teachers who *only* have experience in classical voice pedagogy, and who are employed to teach musical theatre voice without any intervening training in CCM or music theatre singing could be considered reckless,[24] their practice potentially "deleterious to vocal health".[25] This statement might sound alarmist; however, it is important to consider the considerable differences between technical production of classical singing compared to CCM singing. This is yet another example of the "tension … between the competing demands of the academy and the profession",[26] in this case, between voice pedagogy within the academy and the requirements of the musical theatre discipline.

The specifics of voice function in CCM and musical theatre singing: An overview from selected research

How sound is functionally embodied in the singer during a performance is important tacit knowledge teachers bring to their practice because there are considerable differences in voice production elements between CCM and classical singing. Teachers might look to private pedagogical methods for specific training in CCM singing, but they may also look to emerging voice science. Air flow, air pressure, vocal fold closure, resonance, and articulation requirements can vary dramatically between CCM styles. Most CCM research focuses on understanding the resonant properties and physiological functioning of the belt voice or relates to comparisons between musical theatre belt voice and classical voice production. These studies may be useful for classical voice teachers learning how to train students for music theatre singing.

This section outlines some studies on singing in CCM and musical theatre genres. These are separated into research examining the elements of breath, phonation and registration, resonance, and articulation. This separation is somewhat artificial as the singing voice is a unified system where changes in one element of the singing voice can impact on another element of a sung performance.[27] There is a considerably less research into specific CCM genres when compared to the volume of research conducted on classical music singing, and there is more voice science research conducted into the function of music theatre voice compared with research into other CCM genres.

Singing voice research has debunked the historically popular theory that training in the classical tradition is appropriate training for all singing genres. For example, it has been acknowledged that air pressure and flow for CCM singers requires a different approach to that used by classical singers.[28] While there has been considerable research into the specific production of belt singing, which is found in both musical theatre and CCM genres, this research has been performed using participants who are musical theatre performers rather than performers of CCM genres. Scientific-based research into vocal production of genres such as folk, R&B, and hip hop are largely missing from the literature.

Breathing and CCM singing

While there is a large body of work dedicated to exploring breathing in classical singing, there is significantly less research on breathing strategies for CCM singers.[29] The diversity of style requirements in CCM singing means that the breath pressure and flow rate may change from style to style, from song to song within a style, and even within a song to serve the expressivity of the lyric: "Active exhalation is required during skilled speaking and singing, but in wildly different degrees depending on the vocal volume need for the expressive purposes at hand".[30] A performer's individual voice production and physicality also needs to be taken into consideration. Emotional stimulus impacts breathing co-ordination,[31] and pop, R&B, and music theatre singers may be dancing at the same time as singing which further influences their respiratory output during performance.[32]

One study compared five professional music theatre singers and five professional opera performers and discovered that male music theatre singers exhibited higher subglottal pressure than classical male singers.[33] In a study of six singers, a comparison of soul and music theatre singing styles demonstrated higher subglottal pressure in soul singing than music theatre singing.[34] Six professional country singers were found to have higher subglottal pressures when singing compared to subglottal pressures of opera singers.[35] Another single subject study investigating changes in the singer's voice transitioning form opera, to pop, jazz, and blues found similar subglottal pressure to speech production in jazz and pop, and a higher subglottal pressure in blues singing.[36]

Belting and breath

Belt is a voice function found in many CCM styles, including music theatre. Belt is generally said to have a low breath flow and high sub glottal pressure, and utilises stabilisation of the ribcage using the external intercostal muscles.[37] There is no consensus on the most appropriate approach to teaching belters breathing skills for singing and one study found a diverse approach to breathing was used by six professional singers when belting.[38] Studies into music theatre or other CCM singing often compare classical and CCM singers to examine breathing differences between the genres. A study which found belted sounds had a high subglottal pressure when compared with classical singing was only performed on one subject, but the authors considered the sound to be typical of belt singing.[39] A later single subject study into different types of belting found different subglottal pressures, that "heavy" belting had high subglottal pressures, but that "brassy" and "ringy" belting had similar subglottal pressures to classical singing.[40]

The above studies into breathing and belt singing need to be placed into context of the way the vocal folds themselves work during belting. It is not only the characteristics of the air flow and pressure which create the singing sound, but the way that the vocal folds vibrate and create sound as air passes through them which generate appropriate sound.

Registration

Singing voice registration is concerned with the functionality of the voice at the source of the sound, the vocal folds. While registration is a complex physiological and acoustic experience for the singer, appropriate registration can determine style authenticity for the listener. For example, registrational differences are one of the first things a listener might hear and understand as different between a classical soprano and a music theatre belter singing on similar pitches. Inappropriate registration may be the difference between booking a contract and walking away from an audition empty-handed. For example, the different use of female chest and head registers is "the defining difference between female music theater and classical singing".[41] Understanding registration and how to address registrational coordination is of vital importance to the teaching of all singing voice styles, but understanding the specific registrational differences between CCM and classical voice is essential to teaching CCM and musical theatre singing.

Resonance

Resonance refers to the acoustic filtering of the vocal sound once it has passed the vocal folds as the sound wave moves through the air-filled spaces of the vocal tract. As a moveable resonator, the vocal tract "shapes" these sound waves according to the singer's desired timbre, or tone quality. The way the resonating tract is shaped by the singer interacts with the sound wave coming out of the body and assists to create the timbre of a sung sound, for example, boosting, or muffling, a sung note.

Laryngeal position also has an impact on the acoustic properties of a sound. The larynx is a cartilaginous structure which may be low, high, or stay in a stable, speech-like position. Laryngeal position is a function of vocal style—in general terms, classical singing uses a lowered laryngeal position.[42] CCM singers often have a neutral or higher laryngeal position.[43] Low laryngeal position lengthens the vocal tract which results in a boost to low frequencies in the voice. This can create what is perceived as a "warmer" tone.[44] A higher larynx position shortens the vocal tract boosting higher frequencies in the sound waves produced by the vocal folds. This can produce a "brighter" tone. However, in one study a variety of laryngeal positions was observed in music theatre performers producing mix and belt,[45] indicating that individual variability in laryngeal position might be more acceptable in musical theatre singing than in classical singing.

The singer's formant is a cluster of acoustic energy at around 3,000 Hz which the singer may experience as "ring", or an acoustic boost to the singing voice.[46] This is important in classical voice training as the singer needs this formant to project over an orchestra and into a large acoustic space. Development of the singer's formant may not be perceived as important in the CCM singing studio, however "despite the use of personal amplification on the musical theater stage, a ring in the voice is desired" in elite belters in musical theatre.[47] Belting is often perceived as loud, and loudness measurements in belt voice increases as the pitch increases, but there is also an increase in spectral energy at around 4,000 Hz in elite belters, with a rise in first and second formants.[48] Should this quality be desired in any kind of amplified music (including musical theatre) it can be also added by the sound technician at the mixing desk.

Properties of belt

A 2010 study attempted to describe the phonatory and resonance properties of different belt sub-styles (described as heavy, brassy, speech-like, ringy, and nasal) with only one participant singing in each of these sub-styles.[49] This research found that with this subject a higher first formant in the belted sounds was found in the performer when compared with the same performer's classical voice production. Further, the subglottal pressure was highest in heavy belting, lowest in classical voice production, with ringy and brassy belted sounds being produced having a subglottal pressure closer to classical than heavy belting. Belt has an increased closed quotient (how long in a vibratory pattern the vocal folds remain closed) compared to classical singing.[50]

A study examining both physiological and acoustic characteristics of the female musical theatre voice in belt and legit singing, confirmed that belt is produced using mechanism 2 (more commonly referred to as chest register).[51] This study also confirmed the increased closed quotient of the vocal folds present in belt, when compared with legit singing, and that belt singing requires a development of chest register, or mechanism 2, to higher pitches to support belt production. The researchers suggest that differences between belt sub-styles may be due to adjustment in the vocal tract rather than the laryngeal mechanism.[52]

A shortening of the vocal tract, through various muscular adjustments (the raising of the larynx, increased jaw opening) helps create the bright timbre associated with belting.[53] Acoustically speaking, in voice science belt has been accompanied by a "strong F1[first formant] tracking of H2 [the second harmonic] above the normal frequency of F1 for the vowels in question".[54] A recent study suggests that in higher belt notes, a variety of acoustic strategies are being used by professional singers,[55] confirming the earlier study[56] that belt is produced in individual ways depending on the performer's singing strategies.

The diversity of CCM styles means that each style may contain different types of belted sounds which are considered authentic and appropriate. Further, not all CCM styles are belted, and those singers who use belt do not generally use it for the entire duration of a song. Belt is often used to express heightened emotions in the chorus and/or bridge sections within a song. Additionally, mixing desks can now enhance and supply many acoustic permutations once only produced by a singer's unique sound.

Articulation

Articulation is the way in which the sounds we hear as vowels and consonants are formulated into words. Articulation is both an element of voice functionality and a matter of stylistic appropriateness. Sundberg discusses articulation as the "manoeuvres made in order to adjust the vocal tract during phonation"[57] while McKinney discusses articulation in terms of the nature of consonants and the nature of vowels.[58] Bozeman distinguishes between articulation as "the shaping and tuning of the vocal tract" and "how the tongue, lips, jaw, and other speech organs are involved in the production of consonant sounds".[59] Articulation strategies vary between different singing styles. Traditional music theatre singing requires clear diction for speech-like patterning in the singing style, and articulators need to be trained appropriately.[60]

Apart from the considerable differences in articulation between classical singing and musical theatre, there are different articulation conventions between varying CCM styles. Vowel shapes for jazz may be very different to vowel shapes for country. Rock and pop styles may have a more relaxed articulation than musical theatre singing. Muscles of articulation include the many muscles that make up the tongue, lips, soft palate, and pharynx (the back of the throat), and the muscles which move the mouth—those attached to the jaw.[61] Some CCM singing requires very strong articulatory skills (e.g. rap) while others do not have clarity of lyric as their primary concern.

Why are these differences in voice production important?

A change to one element of the singing voice may impact on the performance of another part of the singing voice. For example, an increase in air flow may cause the vocal folds to close more firmly in response, resulting in more thyroarytenoid muscle involvement in the sound, which may lead to a chest register dominant singing sound. A "low breath" common in classical voice production, also called diaphragmatic breathing, may engage some degree of "tracheal pull", where the trachea, and therefore the larynx, may be pulled downwards in concert with the inhalation.[62] The cricothyroid muscle is contracted more vigorously when the diaphragm is in a low position, which can indicate a dominant head register.[63] For female classical singers, this muscular response is appropriate. The lowered larynx combined with head register is most often heard in female classical music and makes this type of breathing a possible pathway to appropriate classical sound. However, the opposite may be true for CCM singers. CCM styles often use a neutral to high laryngeal position and, most importantly for belters, require a thyroarytenoid-dominant (chest register) engagement. This is an example of the extent to which the elements of voice production interact, and how applying a methodology of classical voice style to CCM styles may result in less-than-optimal results. A "one size fits all" approach to singing may not useful.[64] CCM singing voice teachers need to know that classical vocal technique can be inappropriate and may be "deleterious" to a CCM singer's vocal health,[65] that "healthy singing is not just classical singing",[66] and that "each new style – or musical content requires a unique pedagogy".[67]

Classical singing as a deep structure in the employment of musical theatre singing teachers

There are statements by voice pedagogy professional bodies, the clearly different vocal production sounds of contemporary and musical theatre, and scientific research indicating that musical theatre and contemporary singing have different pedagogical requirements to classical singing. However, the presumption that a performance degree in classical singing is an appropriate foundation to being able to teach musical theatre styles continues to hold credence within both specific sectors of academia and the voice pedagogy community. A job advertisement for a musical theatre voice teacher in a US university stated: "Successful candidates should possess a demonstrated record of teaching excellence and the ability to coach students in a wide range of musical theatre styles from golden age to modern and pop/rock while instilling a solid foundation of classical technique".[68] That advertisements like this are still being posted indicates the significant and widespread lack of acknowledgement within academia that "a vocal mechanism trained in that [classical] technique does not automatically nor easily reconfigure to produce sounds that are typical stylistic requirements of CCM repertoire".[69]

There is a general expectation that students who are educated within higher education receive expert standards of tuition to prepare them for the professions. Whether this education is in critical thinking, the professions of law, medicine, and economics, or the creative and performing arts, a deep structure and *signature* of a pedagogy are those assumptions that define the best way to pass on knowledge and know-how to students. In my research I found that one of these deep structures was an assumption surrounding classical voice training in academia as a foundation for teaching of other styles. Despite the claims evident within the literature, and experiences of musical theatre voice teachers themselves about the distinctive requirements of musical theatre singing, which include CCM genres, there remains within HME a broad assumption that a classical voice performance qualification is acceptable and provides the necessary skills and resources a teacher needs to teach within the musical theatre discipline. This has implications when considerations of expertise are applied to voice teaching.

Despite literature explaining CCM and musical theatre singing pedagogy, it appears that an educational background gaining deep, long-term expertise in classical voice production, followed by short course training (2–9 days) in CCM and musical theatre singing can be enough to make a classical voice teacher employable in HME. The opposite would be unthinkable—a contemporary voice teacher taking a short course in classical voice production being considered expert enough to teach classical voice within a university setting. There is a chasm between what the industry expects a student to learn, and the expertise and experiences of teachers HME deems appropriate to teach musical theatre voice students. While I acknowledge that this situation is slowly changing, it remains that university positions continue to be filled by teachers employed to teach musical theatre whose educational background is fully formed by classical singing.

Notes

1 Interview transcription, University M.
2 Ibid.
3 Interview transcription, University V.
4 Interview data was transcribed and de-identified. Teachers were identified by A, B, or C, etc., plus the alphabetical indicator of their university. For example, teacher A at university G was referred to as AG.
5 Interview transcription, University T.
6 Bennett, 2009; Bennett et al., 2015; Bennett & Bridgestock, 2015; Bridgestock, 2005; Bridgestock, 2011; Bridgestock, 2012; Bridgestock et al., 2015; Brown, 2007; Comunian et al., 2011; Comunian et al., 2014; Throsby & Hollister, 2003.
7 Bennett, 2009.
8 Interview transcription, University T.
9 Interview transcription, University V.
10 Ibid.
11 Ibid.
12 Daniel & Parkes, 2015; Watling et al., 2013.
13 Ibid.
14 Interview transcription AT.
15 Ibid.
16 Interview transcription AG.
17 Interview transcription CV.
18 Interview transcription, University T.
19 Ibid.
20 Interview transcription, University V.
21 Interview transcription, University G.
22 Interview transcription, University X.
23 Bartlett, 2010.
24 I want to be clear this does not in any way reflect my views on the participants of the study, many of whom had taken further training in musical theatre and/or CCM pedagogical training.

25 Bartlett, 2010, p. 227.
26 Shulman, 2005, p. 53.
27 I enjoy the musings of the editors of *Bodymind and voice: Foundations of voice education* (Thurman and Welch, 2000) as they consider the complexity of singing. Their approach is expansive and allows for acknowledgment of the singer as a human being with all the complexities associated with the interaction of physiological, psychological, biological, and sociological concerns. I do feel, at heart, that artificially separating these processes and studying them is interesting and useful, but nowhere near the whole picture of what is going on either when we sing, or when we teach singing.
28 American Academy of Teachers of Singing, 2008; Bartlett, 2010; Cleveland, 1998; Fisher et al., 2014; Zangger Borch & Sundberg, 2010.
29 Fisher et al., 2014; LeBorgne & Rosenberg, 2014.
30 Thurman et al., 2000, p. 349.
31 Pettersen & Björkner, 2007.
32 LeBorgne & Rosenberg, 2014; Sliiden et al., 2017.
33 Björkner, 2006.
34 Hallqvist et al., 2016.
35 Cleveland et al., 1996.
36 Thalén & Sundberg, 2001.
37 Bozeman, 2013.
38 Sundberg & Thalén, 2014.
39 Sundberg, 1993.
40 Sundberg et al., 2010.
41 Hall, 2014.
42 Kirkpatrick & McLester, 2012.
43 Bartlett, 2010; Guzman et al., 2014; Riggs, 1998.
44 While the lowered larynx is often associated with the perception of a "warmer" timbre by classical singers, in my own studio practice CCM singers often associated the sounds produced in chest register as "warm" and head register as "bright". In literature "bright" and "warm" timbres are often defined by those writers who have been associated with classical pedagogy and performance. These differences in perceptual qualities may be another element of confusion teaching when CCM singers with classical pedagogical approaches. This would be an interesting research topic!
45 LoVetri et al., 1999.
46 Thurman & Welch, 2000.
47 DeLeo LeBorgne et al., 2009, p. 685.
48 DeLeo LeBorgne et al., 2009.
49 Sundberg et al., 2010.
50 Interestingly, the perceptual qualities of ringy, brassy, and nasal were less likely to be classified by an expert panel as the participant

intended, in particular ringy was misclassified by an expert panel in the majority of cases. Heavy and speech-like were easily classified by the panel. As a side note, from this study it is not clear whether the panel's understanding of what each sound of the terms was intended to portray was checked by the researchers:

As the experiment was run on one single subject only, it was important to evaluate the examples of the various vocal sub-styles recorded. This was done in terms of a listening test with eight experts. The experts were all active as professional teachers of singing in these styles and thus thoroughly acquainted with the styles concerned.

The perceptual misidentification of sounds may have been a semantic issue due to different teachers calling different sounds by different names despite being expert and familiar with the styles. Terminology disagreements and misunderstandings are not uncommon in voice pedagogy.

51 Bourne & Garnier, 2012.
52 Bourne, 2016.
53 Again, I have had CCM students comment that to them belting is "warm" and head register dominant singing is "bright", the opposite of how these perceptual terms are used here. Perception-based terminology used in the singing studio can be fraught with misunderstandings.
54 Bozeman, 2013, p. 68.
55 Flynn et al., 2020.
56 LoVetri et al., 1999.
57 Sundberg, 1987, p. 93.
58 McKinney, 1994.
59 Bozeman, 2013, p. 104.
60 LeBorgne & Rosenberg, 2014; Melton, 2007.
61 McCoy, 2012.
62 Sundberg et al., 1993.
63 Ibid.
64 Bartlett, 2010.
65 Ibid., p. 227.
66 Bunch, 2006, p. 63.
67 O'Bryan & Harrison, 2014, p. 3.
68 University of Memphis, 2019.
69 American Academy of Teachers of Singing, 2008, p. 3.

References

American Academy of Teachers of Singing. (2008). *In support of Contemporary Commercial Music (nonclassical) voice pedagogy*. www.americanacademyofteachersofsinging.org/assets/articles/CCMVoicePedagogy.pdf

Bartlett, I. (2010). One size doesn't fit all: Tailored training for contemporary commercial singers. In S. Harrison (Ed.), *Perspectives on teaching singing: Australian pedagogues sing their stories* (pp. 227–243). Australian Academic Press.

Bennett, D. (2009). Academy and the real world: Developing realistic notions of career in the performing arts. *Arts & Humanities in Higher Education, 8*(3), 309–327.

Bennett, D., & Bridgestock, R. (2015). The urgent need for career preview: Student expectations and graduate realities in music and dance. *International Journal of Music Education, 33*(3), 263–267.

Bennett, D., Richardson, S., Mahat, M., Coates, H., MacKinnon, P., & Schmidt, L. (2015, July 6–9). *Navigating uncertainty and complexity: Higher education and the dilemma of employability*. Paper presented at the 38th HERDSA Annual International Conference, Melbourne.

Björkner, E. (2006). Musical theatre and opera singing—Why so different? A study of subglottal pressure, voice source and formant frequency characteristics. *Journal of Voice, 22*(5), 533–540.

Bourne, T. (2016). Perceptual, acoustic and physiological characteristics of musical theatre singing. [Doctoral Thesis]. Sydney University.

Bourne, T., & Garnier, M. (2012). Physiological and acoustic characteristics of the female music theatre voice. *Journal of the Acoustical Society of America, 131*, 1586–1596.

Bozeman, K. (2013). *Practical vocal acoustics: Pedagogical applications for teachers and singers*. Pendragon Press.

Bridgestock, R. (2005). Australian artists, starving and well-nourished: What can we learn from the prototypical protean career? *Australian Journal of Career Development, 14*(3), 40–48.

Bridgestock, R. (2011). Skills for creative industries graduate success. *Education + Training, 53*(1), 9–26.

Bridgestock, R. (2012). Not a dirty word: Arts entrepreneurship and higher education. *Arts & Humanities in Higher Education, 12*(2–3), 122–137.

Bridgestock, R., Goldsmith, B., Rodgers, J., & Hearn, G. (2015). Creative graduate pathways within and beyond the creative industries. *Journal of Education and Work, 28*(4), 333–345. doi: 10.1080/13639080.2014.997682

Brown, R. (2007). Enhancing student employability? Current practice and student experiences in HE performing arts. *Arts & Humanities in Higher Education, 6*(1), 28–49. doi: 10.1177/1474022207072198

Bunch Dayme, M. (2006). An argument for whole body and holistic approaches to research in singing. *Journal of Singing, 63*(1), 59–64.

Cleveland, T. (1998). A comparison of breath management strategies in classical and nonclassical singers: Part 3. *Journal of Singing, 55*(2), 53–55.

Cleveland, T., Stone, E., Sundberg, J., & Iwarsson, J. (1996). Estimated subglottal pressure in six professional country singers. *Journal of Voice, 11*(4), 403–409.
Comunian, R., Faggian, A., & Jewell, S. (2011). Winning and losing in the creative industries: An analysis of creative graduates' career opportunities across creative disciplines. *Cultural Trends, 20*(3–4), 291–308.
Comunian, R., Faggian, A., & Jewell, S. (2014). Embedding arts and humanities in the creative economy: The role of graduates in the UK. *Environment and Planning C: Government and Policy, 32*, 426–450. doi: 10.1068/c11153r
Daniel, R., & Parkes, K. (2015). The apprentice to master journey: Exploring tertiary music instrument teachers' reflections on their experiences as learner. *Journal of Arts and Humanities, 4*(3), 52–63.
DeLeo LeBorgne, W., Lee, L. Stemple, J., & Bush, H., (2009). Perceptual findings on the Broadway belt voice. *Journal of Voice, 24*(6), 678–689.
Fisher, J., Kayes, G., & Popeil, L. (2014). Pedagogy of different sung genres. In G. Welch, J. Nix, & D. Howard (Eds.), *The Oxford handbook of singing.* doi: 10.1093/oxfordhb/9780199660773.013.005
Flynn, A., Trudeau, J., & Johnson, A. (2020). Acoustic comparison of lower and higher belt ranges in professional Broadway actresses. *Journal of Voice, 34*(3), 410–414. doi: 10.1016/j.jvoice.2018.10.006
Guzman, M., Barros, M., Espinoza, F., Herrera, A., Parra, D., Muñoz, D., & Lloyd, A. (2014). Laryngoscopic, acoustic, perceptual, and functional assessment of voice in rock singers. *Folia Phoniatrica et Logopedica, 65.* 248–256. doi: 10.1159/000357707
Hall, K. (2014). *So you want to sing music theater.* Rowman & Littlefield.
Hallqvist, H., Lã, F., & Sundberg, J., (2016). Soul and musical theatre: A comparison of two vocal styles. *Journal of Voice, 31*(2), 229–235.
Kirkpatrick, A., & McLester, J. (2012). Teaching lower laryngeal position with EMG biofeedback. *Journal of Singing, 68*(3), 253–260.
LeBorgne, W., & Rosenberg, M. D. (2014). *The vocal athlete.* Plural.
LoVetri, J., Lesh, S., & Woo, P. (1999). Preliminary study on the ability of trained singers to control the intrinsic and extrinsic laryngeal musculature. *Journal of Voice, 13*(2), 219–226.
McCoy, S. (2012). *Your voice: An inside view.* Inside View Press.
McKinney, J. (1994). *The diagnosis and correction of vocal faults: A manual for teachers of singing and for choir directors.* Genevox Music Group.
Melton, J. (2007). *Singing in musical theatre: The training of singers and actors.* Allworth.O'Bryan, J., & Harrison, S. (2014). Prelude: Positioning singing pedagogy in the twenty-first century. In S. Harrison & J. O'Bryan (Eds.), *Teaching singing in the 21st century* (pp. 1–9). Springer. doi: 10.1007/978-97-017-8851-9
Pettersen, V., & Bjorkoy, K. (2007). Consequences from emotional stimulus on breathing for singing. *Journal of Voice, 23*(3), 295–303.

Riggs, S. (1998). *Singing for the stars*. Alfred.
Shulman, L. (2005). Signature pedagogies in the professions. *Daedalus, 134*(3), 52–59.
Sliiden, T., Beck, S., & MacDonald, I. (2017). An evaluation of the breathing strategies and maximum phonation time in musical theater performers during controlled performance tasks. *Journal of Voice, 31*(2), 253.e.1–253.e.11.
Sundberg, J. (1987). *The science of the singing voice*. Northern Illinois Press.
Sundberg, J., Gramming, P., & LoVetri, J. (1993). Comparisons of pharynx, source, formant and pressure characteristics in operatic and musical theatre singing. *Journal of Voice, 7*(4), 301–310.
Sundberg, J., & Thalén, M. (2014). Respiratory and acoustical differences between belt and neutral style of singing. *Journal of Voice, 29*(4), 418–425. doi: 10.1080/140154301753207458
Sundberg, J., Thalén, M., & Popeil, L. (2010). Substyles of belting: Phonatory and resonatory characteristics. *Journal of Voice, 26*(1), 44–50. doi: 10.1016/j.jvoice.2010.10.007Throsby, D., & Hollister, V. (2003). *Don't give up your day job: An economic study of professional artists in Australia*. The Australia Council.
Thalén, M., & Sundberg, J. (2001). Describing different styles of singing: A comparison of a female singer's voice source in "Classical", "Pop", "Jazz" and "Blues". *Logopedics Phoniatrics Vocology, 26*(2), 82–93, doi: 10.1080/140154301753207458
Thurman, L., Theimer, A., Welch, G., Grefsheim, E., & Feit, P., (2000). Creating breathflow for skilled speaking and singing. In L. Thurman, G. Welch, (Eds.), *Bodymind & voice: Foundations of voice education* (pp. 339–355). The VoiceCare Network.
Thurman, L., & Welch, G. (2000). *Bodymind & voice: Foundations of voice education*. The VoiceCare Network.
University of Memphis Career Opportunities, (2019, December 18). *Assistant professor in musical theatre voice*. https://workforum.memphis.edu/postings/24394
Watling, C., Driessen, E., van der Vleuten, C., Vanstone, M., & Lingard, L. (2013). Music lessons: Revealing medicine's learning culture through a comparison with that of music. *Medical Education, 47*, 842–850.
Zangger Borch, D., & Sundberg, J. (2010). Some phonatory and resonatory characteristics of the rock, pop, soul, and Swedish dance bands styles of singing. *Journal of Voice, 25*(5), 532–537. doi: 10.1016/j.jvoice.2010.07.014

5 Deep structures of voice pedagogy in universities in the United States

The one-to-one model

Deep structures in pedagogical models are those "assumptions about how best to impart a certain body of knowledge and know-how".[1] The first and most obvious deep structure of singing teaching in higher education is the assumption that the private, one-to-one pedagogical model is the most appropriate way of teaching singing. It is a tradition in voice pedagogy that the knowledge and know-how of singing is typically passed on through the one-to-one teaching modality. This has emerged from the conventions of classical voice teaching and the master–apprentice model within HME.[2] Other ways of teaching voice exist and were demonstrated in the lessons observed in this study, with a prominent example being that of paired lessons. Group singing classes were also observed in two institutions, as were masterclass structures in most programmes. However, most musical theatre singing lessons observed in this study aligned with existing literature into classical voice pedagogy, i.e., that private singing lessons in universities is largely taught through the traditional one-to-one delivery model.[3]

Under these conditions, the one-to-one modality of lessons supports, reinforces, and reproduces a teacher's (and, by extension, the academy's) individualised, idiosyncratic approach to pedagogy, reflecting the history and evolution of the one-to-one voice lesson within the HME environment.[4] The architecture of the teacher's studio lends itself to the reproduction of this modality, this private space providing teachers with autonomy over practices and approaches to lesson delivery. Specifically,

DOI: 10.4324/9781003332572-5

each of the teachers encountered for this study had experienced one-to-one lessons in their own training background, and it was something of an unquestioned assumption that this mode of voice training, supported by studio classes where students could practice performance skills in front of their peers, stood as the "appropriate" modality of teaching to pass on the skills and know-how of singing in musical theatre. It is the *assumption* that one-to-one is the appropriate way to pass on knowledge and know-how about musical theatre singing that makes this a *deep* structure, as well as a surface structure. Teachers reproduced the pedagogy of singing using the modality they had experienced in their own lives. While these practices may have been refined and altered in certain ways, it remained a recognisable approach to pedagogy, the *signature* of the one-to-one singing lesson, and pervasive across institutions.

What can you sing? Performance backgrounds of musical theatre singing teachers

The second deep structure generated from the data analysis was that of the teacher as a performer. Teachers of singing are expected and assumed to have performance experience in their background, and that this performance experience is considered vital to imparting knowledge about how to become a performer. Most employment advertisements for voice teaching jobs in HME require the applicant to have performance experience. While some advertisements specify a national or international level of experience and profile, others require less extensive performance experience. During the interview process this may involve the candidate performing a concert or recital of work to prove their performance ability, despite being employed to teach, and not to perform. During the Covid pandemic it became commonplace for video evidence of recent performances to verify the applicant's performance skills. In this study, most participant teachers had professional performance experiences, although at a variety of levels and in a variety of styles. Participants mostly had musical theatre performance experience, although two teachers noted that their experience in this genre was limited to legit-style musical theatre productions which suited their vocal training and singing style. Others commented that their performance experience came exclusively from student productions with limited professional performance experience in either opera

Voice pedagogy in universities in the United States 79

or musical theatre. Some participants had highly valued Broadway performance experience and considerable national tour exposure in both opera and musical theatre.

What hadn't teachers performed?

The deep structure within voice pedagogy lessons I observed is the assumption that teachers are performers, and it is through their performance experiences and backgrounds that the embodiment, the knowledge, and know-how of performance, is passed on to students. Participants' performance skills were often associated with classical and musical theatre voice styles. The performance of pop, rock, country, and other CCM genres were rare in the performance practices of the participant teachers who took part in this study. Teachers were largely trained in classical voice singing, and generally had limited to no experience of performance in the CCM genres which are becoming ubiquitous in the industry. The assumption here is that performance experience is relevant, no matter what kind of performance it is. Classical performance experience has its own conventions and aesthetics which are entirely different to performing in musical theatre. Musical theatre performance conventions are also very different to the ways in which CCM performers experience singing and performance, with different aesthetics and embodiment. Ironically, despite performance experience being highly valued, many participants did not have performance experience in the styles they were being employed to teach.

Two participants had backgrounds as music directors and did not consider themselves vocal performers at all. One commented that they had "never sung on the stage" despite doing a vocal performance major in a master's degree. The other teacher with a music direction background experienced a great fear of performing, had taken voice class for a semester during undergraduate training to overcome the fear, but rarely sang. Discussing a memorable cabaret performance, the participant shared:

> I think I just had enough gin and tonic in me that I sort of lost that little bit of fear ... and I sang and the earth didn't swallow me up ... I still sing under duress, I still have that, you know, I'm more comfortable singing from the piano.[5]

Interestingly, for these participants their music direction skills and ability and experience in providing voice coaching and singing lessons was considered enough of an appropriate background to gain entry to academic employment as a musical theatre singing voice teacher. Experience as a music director was the *only* exemption observed in the data set to the performance background requirement for employment as a singing teacher in higher education. Both musical directors had studied voice pedagogy extensively and were highly experienced and expert at teaching musical theatre singing students musical theatre singing styles. This expertise and training, like the other participants, came after their university-based education.

Related to the training background of teachers, most of the teachers were notably most confident talking about their legit-style performance backgrounds. Participants that did have CCM performance experience (other than musical theatre legit or belt-style singing) qualified singing these styles in some way. A participant whose professional experience included performances at the highest level in classical music,[6] explored performing CCM genres:

R: What about performing pop/rock/country? Have you performed those styles?

AM: Um, a little bit. Only in sort of cabaret settings ... not, not legitimately. I had a band for a little while here, for about a year. It was basically like two people doing singer-songwritery (sic) stuff with harmony. ... and it was sort of I think a contemporary folk sound, so it's not, tremendously different from my default way of singing anyway. Um, my voice is totally dressed down from how I was trained. So, the way that I teach now and the way that I prefer to sing now is much more plain ... And I feel like it's my true sound and the classical sound was like an affectation.[7]

Interestingly, the experimentation in CCM and musical theatre singing resulted in a changed vocal identity. This teacher found an emerging sense of authenticity in their singing voice through CCM-specific retraining and performance. This experimentation with contemporary folk singing was not considered legitimate performance experience of CCM singing by the teacher.

Another participant, whose training was entirely classical at university and who performed in national tours of opera productions prior to teaching, learnt to transition into performing musical theatre styles after graduation. When discussing other CCM genres in the studio and performance, she experimented with:

> A slight jazz thing, a slight twang for a country song, but *I* could never really approach a rock or, I mean a really contemporary rock/pop sound ... I myself, could not one, demonstrate, not be able to demonstrate and two, would **never** be hired to sing that rep.[8]

This teacher was extremely clear about the demarcation between classical and contemporary voice production. They were aware of their inability to produce a contemporary sound with an authenticity which could be considered professional standard, despite a career in theatre and performance background in a touring opera company.

One participant had sung "a whole broad mix of stuff from pop to a lot of musical theatre"[9] in their career working on cruise ships. Unfortunately, their classical training was not appropriate for singing these styles and left their voice "knotted" up. They described frustration at a concert performance where they were unable to authentically sing a song in pop style. After teaching musical theatre singing in academia for many years, the teacher was able to take professional development courses in CCM singing. They compared their earlier professional career experience with the confidence they now feel after taking CCM technical training. In fact, their CCM training had a positive impact when performing both classical and contemporary styles: "five years ago I couldn't do the things vocally I do now. Couldn't even come close to that ... I do I feel so much more freedom to go from really low to really high".[10]

Participant teachers' lack of experience in CCM performance styles is hardly surprising considering the years of classical training most participants had undertaken. Schindler[11] has discussed the values that classical voice teachers who are also performers bring to the voice studio, including a tacit understanding of what it is to be a performer, the type of energy, effort, practice, and skill required to perform in the industry at the professional level and the mindsets which are appropriate to life as a performer. I observed that a teacher's ability to perform and demonstrate musical theatre and CCM genres resulted in more specificity, understanding, and confidence in teaching practices in these styles to prepare students for a performance career.

Performance practice differences between classical singing and contemporary singing styles

Chapter 4 laid out selected technical differences between CCM singing and classical singing as reported by research into the singing voice and singing styles. However, it is not only the technical differences which matter when performing CCM and musical theatre music. Performance skills in classical and operatic singing are also defined by conventions and practices which are quite different to musical theatre and CCM performances. Audition processes and concert performances in the classical world generally requires more formal attire than is usual in musical theatre. Musical theatre performers are triple threats and must sing, dance, and act to be considered appropriately skilled for the industry. Classical performers may experience some movement and acting classes within their training, but there is not the same emphasis placed on these performance aspects as there is in musical theatre study. CCM singers must embody the music in specific ways to create the appropriate aesthetic, while classical singers often perform with minimal physical movement. The clothing worn by CCM singers is considerably different to the clothing worn by classical performers. Even performance career age is different in these two worlds—classical performers take a long time to train their instruments and often do not embark on a professional career until after they have had master's level training. Musical theatre performers are expected to be ready to perform professionally and be fully developed triple threats as soon as possible. The aesthetic requirements and social structures of musical theatre and CCM singing are different to those which are expected in the classical world.

To put the nuances of performance style between genres into perspective, classical voice pedagogues might scoff at contemporary performers' attempts to perform classical pieces. Social media critiques of Michael Bolton performing "Nessun Dorma", or Barbra Streisand singing "Lascia ch'io pianga" are specific performances I recall being eviscerated by classical colleagues. This is because classical singing is not only about the repertoire itself, but also an artistic and technical way of singing developed over many years of training which imbues the singer with a culturally specific and technically appropriate style of performance. Additionally, there are stylistic nuances within classical voice training—the singer who performs Handel has a different skillset and voice type to the singer who performs Wagner. The same can be said of the huge variety of singing styles encompassed by musical theatre. The highest standards of musical theatre and other contemporary-styled singing performances can require specific functional and artistic skills, which take time to develop in the same way that classical voice technique requires long term training. It is questionable whether teachers who spend years training in classical programmes, developing classical voice function and style, receive appropriate training within these programmes to learn how to embody the functionality necessary to perform at a professional level of musical theatre, particularly in the many kinds of CCM styles musical theatre now encompasses.

How did teachers navigate the complexity of teaching what they are not trained to do?

While participant teachers brought their performance mindsets and experiences to lessons, there was at times an observed disconnect between the kinds of material teachers themselves embodied, demonstrated, and performed at a professional level, and the repertoire and voice function students are now required to perform. Yes, teachers had a variety of musical theatre experiences prior to their employment, ranging from extensive (Broadway and national tour experience) to minimal (a single college performance in a musical), however the data exposed a considerable lack of performance experience in CCM genres. Further, several participant teachers were only comfortable performing legit-style musical theatre.

Embodiment of performance skills were considered essential to the employment of voice teachers within the university system and was found to be a deep structure of voice pedagogy. These performance skills were considered acceptable for employment in teaching musical theatre singing despite being grounded in the classical aesthetic. In their interviews and in discussions with me, teachers often discussed the need to train into their own voices the specific differences between their classical training and musical theatre singing. A few teachers had worked on training CCM styles and differentiating these styles from musical theatre in their own voices, but this differentiation was not always directly acknowledged, or recognisable in the teaching of lessons. Some teachers relied on their ears to listen and understand the sounds that were being made and tried to work out how students could do these safely—teachers were clearly aware that performing CCM genres with inappropriate function could have negative consequences to a performer's voice.[12]

Teacher embodiment of singing function and style is an implicit structure of voice pedagogy and a performance background is a requirement of employment, yet some teachers were still working out how to embody musical theatre sounds, let alone other CCM sounds:

> She has found herself conflicted as a MT performer. She is a character actor, but often worries about not using classical training in her vowels when performing and feels that this impacts on her ability to act with integrity at times.[13]

Because this study utilised participant observation, in the second week of my visit the teacher in the above note asked me to team teach her students so she could learn from watching my practice. She also asked me to teach her, and my notes from the second lesson reflect how important understanding embodiment of function can be to a teacher and performer:

> Yesterday was a day of lessons from 9am to 5.30pm, and at the end of the day I gave BQ a second lesson. It was a pretty thrilling day in lessons, releasing people's voices—BQ asked me to work with all her students, and we discussed pedagogically what was happening as I worked with them. In BQ's lesson the biggest "aha" moment for her was how little air is required for CCM singing. She was using her "full classical tank" of air to sing, and when I had her speak then sing in exactly the same way in terms of consonant production and airflow her voice gently sat

in a mix and belt very naturally. She was completely blown away as she realized this was why belting had never worked for her—she was using too much air and carrying too much weight in the sound up high because the subglottal pressure was too much for singing CCM. She had a huge revelation—she actually looked like she might faint in the lesson, because she realized she had been trying to address student's difficulty belting with more air and connection to breath, and that was producing all kinds of tensions in the voice. In particular we worked with TQ and released her tongue and her belt went right up to Eb5 immediately. TQ was in tears at the new found freedom in her voice.[14]

This teacher had a degree in musical theatre performance, had performed in musical theatre but had not experienced the embodiment of belting. This led to difficulty understanding the relationship of breath to belting compared to her own classical training in teaching practice. There appears to be a disconnect between the deep structure of the importance of embodied performance experience in the teacher for employment, the surface structure of musical theatre and CCM repertoire, and the performance expectations of musical theatre students. The emotional reactions of the teacher in the above excerpt demonstrates the importance of embodiment and appropriate functional training for style to performers and teachers alike.

Notions of expertise: Performer as teacher?

While performance experience is an implicit structure within expected backgrounds of voice teachers in university faculty, it remains that successful performance careers do not necessarily translate to successful teaching careers, however attractive a performer's profile may be to an educational institution wishing to attract students. The highest-level performers (often signified in job advertisements as "national recognition or Broadway experience required") do not automatically become expert teachers. In a study examining differences between medical training and musical training, music performance students stated unequivocally that instructional ability was valued higher than performance expertise.[15] Capable demonstration was important, but demonstration must be followed by detailed meaningful instruction that helps the student understand how the performance is to be created ... a teacher's virtuosity as a performer might actually have a detrimental effect on his or her teaching capacity ... learners could readily distinguish great teachers from great performers.[16]

While performance experience is always valued, teaching skill is not always signified by a teacher's performance career or fame.[17] Stylistically appropriate and functionally sound demonstration is useful in the private music studio, and in order to perform this demonstration teachers do need to be able to perform styles and functions at a standard appropriate to instruction. However, the ability to demonstrate a singing skill does not need to be at the expense of pedagogical skills and students are acutely aware of the difference between a high-level performer who is also teaching, and a teacher with high-level pedagogical skills.[18] While performers certainly bring valued performance experiences to the teaching studio, students may present these teacher-performers with voice-related issues beyond their experience or understanding if they have not completed advanced education in voice pedagogy.

A complex, nuanced relationship with performance backgrounds

Teachers whose performance backgrounds were mostly classical experienced a complex and nuanced relationship with this style of singing. While acknowledging that the style was not useful for them in their own performance objectives in musical theatre or CCM singing, they were proud of their classical performance skills. They taught students classical repertoire and expected them to learn German, French, or Italian diction to perform this repertoire. Classical singing and "cross over" techniques were taught in most studios, despite the students being enrolled in musical theatre degrees. When transitioning back from teaching classical styles during cross training sessions, linguistic slips often occurred. A teacher's aesthetic preference for classical singing might be made clear by language describing classical singing as sounds of "beauty" and "warmth". In these instances, words describing CCM or musical theatre singing included "harsh", "nasty", and "nasal".

While teachers-accepted classical singing skills were not necessarily going to be replicated in the same way with their musical theatre students, participants often expressed regard for classical singing and pride in their personal performance abilities and achievements. These achievements and abilities were useful to them in terms of credibility and formed the basis (or deep structure) for a career teaching in academia. The teachers found value for students in reproducing these abilities through the teaching of classical repertoire and its associated practices (diction, foreign languages, specific resonant and registrational choices).

Some participants expressed great pride in their background and the resulting ability to "fit in" at voice conferences with classical colleagues. This gave them, particularly younger teachers with doctoral degrees, the ability to speak to classical pedagogues and "bridge the gap" between musical theatre, CCM, and classical voice colleagues. Their classical performance careers, and classical training to master's and doctoral levels gave them access to speak with a sense of authority to those classically trained pedagogues with less experience in the musical theatre and CCM space. There was little reflection about why those teachers whose training and performance background was largely in CCM and musical theatre were absent from academic spaces. The following chapters examine this absence in further detail.

Notes

1 Shulman, 2005, p. 55.
2 Boardman, 1987.
3 King & Nix, 2019; Callaghan, 2010; O'Bryan & Harrison, 2014.
4 O'Bryan & Harrison, 2014.
5 Interview transcription, University X.
6 By performing classical singing at the highest level, here I mean performed at opera theatres such as The Met, Carnegie Hall, Covent Garden, or other highly respected international performance spaces.
7 Interview transcription, University M.
8 Interview transcription, University G.
9 Interview transcription AQ.
10 Ibid.
11 Schindler, 2010.
12 Bartlett, 2010.
13 Reflexive notes, University Q.

14 Ibid.
15 Watling et al., 2013.
16 Ibid., p. 846.
17 See also Persson (1994, 1996).
18 Watling et al., 2013.

References

Bartlett, I. (2010). One size doesn't fit all: Tailored training for contemporary commercial singers. In S. Harrison (Ed.), *Perspectives on teaching singing: Australian pedagogues sing their stories* (pp. 227–243). Australian Academic Press.

Boardman, S. (1987). Voice training for the musical theatre singer. (Doctor of Musical Arts in Voice). Retrieved from ProQuest database. (8722053)

Callaghan, J. (2010). Singing teaching as a profession. In S. Harrison (Eds.), *Perspectives on teaching singing: Australian vocal pedagogues sing their stories* (pp. 13–30). Australian Academic Press.

King, M., & Nix, J. (2019). Conservatory teaching and learning. In G. Welch, D. Howard, & J. Nix (Eds.), *The Oxford handbook of singing* (pp. 689–705). Oxford University Press.

O'Bryan, J., & Harrison, S. (2014). Prelude: Positioning singing pedagogy in the twenty-first century. In S. Harrison & J. O'Bryan (Eds.), *Teaching singing in the 21st century* (pp. 1–9). Springer. doi: 10.1007/978-97-017-8851-9

Persson, R. (1994). Concert musicians as teachers: On good intentions falling short. *European Journal for High Ability*, 5(1), 79–91. doi: 10.1080/0937445940050108

Persson, R. (1996). Studying with a musical maestro: A case study of commonsense teaching in artistic training. *Creativity Research Journal*, 9(1), 33–46.

Schindler, M. (2010). Performers as teachers: A tertiary perspective. In S. Harrison (Ed.), *Perspectives on teaching singing: Australian vocal pedagogues sing their stories* (pp. 31–46). Australian Academic Press.

Shulman, L. (2005). Signature pedagogies in the professions. *Daedalus*, 134(3), 52–59.

Watling, C., Driessen, E., van der Vleuten, C., Vanstone, M., & Lingard, L. (2013). Music lessons: Revealing medicine's learning culture through a comparison with that of music. *Medical Education*, 47, 842–850.

6 Habitus and capitals of musical theatre singing teachers

Habitus: What is it and why does it matter?

Bourdieu contends that personal behaviours, individual decisions, the activation of private "tastes", and the conduct of practice are based on individual actions and beliefs. These actions and beliefs are mediated through culturally negotiated social contexts and histories. Individual actions within a specific field are socially shaped according to strategies designed to position a member of a cultural group (or organisation/institution within a cultural group) in a certain way, and in relation to others. When these individual choices multiply within a group they become "common trends",[1] and present as indicative of a wider social "logic" that orders and makes the social group recognisable. This logic becomes "tacit knowledge that guides individuals to orientate their actions in certain ways"[2] and the learning of this social logic is the process of enculturation into cultural group. Habitus is not a specific entity, but a "thinking tool" for setting out what a culture is, what the ontological characteristics of a cultural group are, and most importantly, how an individual should enact and embody the *sensibilities* of the group. This sensibility frames how an individual within the group behaves and positions themselves, together with and through the "capital" one holds, within the cultural group.

For Bourdieu, social, cultural, and symbolic *capital* provides the point of expression of the habitus. In enacting the behaviours and sensibilities of the group, individuals will recognise certain ways of being, ways of speaking, expressions of style and taste as "appropriate" to the group. The individual's ability to enact their own way of being will result in individuals positioning themselves

DOI: 10.4324/9781003332572-6

and being positioned by a social group. For the purposes of this present argument, Bourdieu's identification of these expressions of habitus work to define how individuals come to enact the practices they do, in line with and according to the sensibilities of the social settings in which they are situated. Habitus "functions below the level of consciousness"[3] and is a useful way of observing the relationship between situations and practices.[4]

Habitus captures the fundamental "elements" that define a cultural group. These elements include the time position of the group within a wider historic time period, its identity characteristics including ethnicity, gender, and class, and its collective sensibilities including prevailing cultural values and discernment of "style". It is considered by Bourdieu to be a "unifying principle" of a specific social or cultural group. The designation of the habitus may appear clear cut, but in reality, habitus is messy and has individual exceptions and subjectivities, and accordingly, not all participants exhibited all characteristics in equal ways. Notably, however, in this study there were enough commonalities across the specific elements of habitus to identify music theatre voice teachers working in higher education as a specific cultural group set within the larger cultural group of singing voice teachers.

> Habitus is both structured and structuring.[5] Habitus is structured by past and present circumstances, such as family upbringing and educational experiences. It is "structuring" in that habitus informs, facilitates, and shapes an individual and/or social group's present and future practices.[6]

While habitus is generally instilled during childhood, there is also a secondary habitus "learned later as one takes on a profession or trade".[7] Habitus is concerned with the way we act, think, feel, and are in the social world. It is embodied and carried with us into social situations and, when combined with capitals, influences both our positioning in a field and our practices.

This chapter examines the habitus, characteristics, and sensibilities of the field of musical theatre voice teachers in academia in the United States through the context of the participants of this study. I draw on the recognisable set of participants' dispositions and backgrounds which illustrated both the musical theatre pedagogical field within academia and the relationship between this cultural group, classical voice pedagogy within academia, and the larger cultural group of general voice pedagogy.

Gender

Out of the 13 participant teachers in this study, 3 were male and 10 were female.[8] While a discussion of the gender characteristics of the voice studio, and the wider field of musical theatre was outside the scope of this project, and this is a small sample of musical theatre voice teachers, the dominance of female identifying teachers in this participant group must be noted. Smith has identified HME's traditionally male-dominant structure and operationalisation.[9] He notes this particularly in relation to executive power structures, gender of teaching faculty and executive staff, and the masculine power dynamic of the master–apprentice mode of delivery. The instrumental disciplines of guitar, bass, and drums "are gendered as 'male' … with vocals (listed last on the website and in the prospectus) being strongly associated with (and far more permissible for) females".[10]

While Smith's study was undertaken at a private popular music institution, rather than musical theatre education provider, the gendering of singing as female *is* reflected in the gender division of voice teachers in the study. This is significant when considering males have a much higher rate of full-time employment in academic institutions in the United States,[11] yet in this discipline (within this admittedly small group of participants) the opposite is true. However, it should be noted that where males were involved as participants in this study, they were always in more senior positions within the faculty than females. This is reflective of research into gender equity in leadership roles and female/male participation in music performance.[12]

While some professional, structuring bodies within the field of voice pedagogy continue to diversify in terms of gender equality within executive bodies, there is an underlying power differential where regular stable income is to be made from the voice teaching profession, that is, within higher education. While the general population of voice teachers in the United States is gendered largely female,[13] in academia it is now closer to parity.[14] Numbers of females involved in higher music education have increased, yet female incomes in the field continue to lag in the United States.[15]

While this particular area of research was outside the scope of my study, international research is ongoing into the ways in which work within university structures is highly gendered, and the ways in which male academics position themselves at an advantage within the system in terms of salary, promotion, and work performance expectations.[16] While there may be a surge towards equality in numbers, real equity in terms of work expectations[17] in voice pedagogy in academia has yet to be extensively researched.

Ethnicity

All teachers who were study participants were identified as white. This is reflective of higher education in the United States, where 76% of all full-time faculty identify as "Caucasian".[18] Many musical theatre schools actively promote diversity within their student cohort, recognising that if ethnic diversity is not represented in the student body, ethnic diversity is not represented on stage and further, future teachers of the discipline will not reflect ethnic diversity. This lack of ethnic diversity among faculty is echoed by historical data collected on those in positions of authority in the theatre industry—in the 2016–2017 Broadway season 95% of directors were identified as Caucasian.[19]

Considering 11 out of 13 participants in this study were trained in classical music programmes but progressed into the musical theatre field, the ethnicity of faculty and students within the cultural group of HME in the United States also needs consideration. Many musical theatre voice teachers are employed by music departments within universities. If the teachers are employed by the theatre department, they are often interviewed by executives within the department or school during the interview process who have come from a classical music background. Music programmes in the United States are dominated by classical music,[20] which has "avoided diversification".[21] The lack of diversity in classical music, the cultural "whiteness" of the field both in the professional arena and in higher education in the United States have been the subject of recent scholarship. In a call to action, Feder and McGill[22] outline in detail the environment created by structural racism experienced by minority performers in the classical music arena. The authors describe hostility experienced by BIPOC performers which is presented as culturally ingrained in both educational and performance institutions which support classical music. Other recent scholarship specifically examines the ways in which higher music education prioritises Western classical music over non-Western classical music through the perpetuation of white supremacy.[23] Students and performers who are not white have experienced micro-aggressions and outright hostility. If this is experienced by students of classical music, attempting to move into this space as an academic to work and teach in such environments without significant cultural change is understandably not an attractive prospect for BIPOC musicians. Classical music programmes have traditionally been welcoming to white students, have taught mostly white students, and so voice teachers who emerge from this system will, in turn, largely be white.

Historic time period

The historic time period within which this study was conducted—between August 2018 and September 2019—is relevant to the training background of the participants. Teachers in the study were educated prior to the recent development of graduate degrees in musical theatre voice pedagogy in the United States[24] (for example, Penn State University's graduate degree began in 2011; Carthage College, 2019; Boston Conservatory, 2020) or a terminal (doctoral) degree specialising in CCM voice pedagogy (Shenandoah Conservatory, 2020). Specialist musical theatre or CCM voice pedagogy graduate degrees (i.e., without also having a classical component) are still not widely available in the United States. Teachers discussed the lack of pedagogical training in styles other than the classical voice they were given during their graduate degrees, resulting in the participants requiring additional education once they encountered the day-to-day skills required in the field of teaching:

> After I finished my doctorate ... my teaching studio really turned toward CCM, and the demand was just huge ... my students wanted to know how to belt ... they needed to belt their faces off, and I didn't have any skills to teach them how to do that, and I didn't know how to do it myself either. So that's when I started taking private lessons to learn how to belt and started studying more formally.[25]

Further, participants discussed the complete lack of knowledge that there were any other options to study singing:

> I didn't even know that (CCM singing) was a thing, really. Um, I certainly didn't know that it was something we could work on in a voice lesson because it just wasn't a thing back then ... I didn't hear people doing CCM in recitals.[26]

The choice to study other styles of music was simply not widely available to this cohort of participants during the period of their education.

A classical-based education is designed to enculturate participants in their formative, educational years into classical music culture, practices, and aesthetics. However, for reasons of economics (teachers needing to teach students who desired to sing CCM styles, and/or wanting to be employed to perform musical theatre styles), aesthetics (personal voice quality not meeting the accepted classical aesthetic, desiring a more "individual" singing sound), and participant desire (wanting to learn to teach and perform musical theatre styles), participant teachers left the classical voice community and entered the musical theatre space.

The deep structure within music theatre voice pedagogy is that voice teachers will have a classical voice degree. This is because in the historic time period of participants' education and training, this is what was available in higher education. While the situation is dynamic, it is very slow to change. Because the bulk of music programmes still focus on classical music performance, this kind of training continues to be privileged over other styles of music performance training.[27] There is an accepted "logic" that classical voice education prepares students for a career in "music" in the United States, even though teachers recognised the contradiction within this institutionalised practice. The logic behind this assumption is, in fact, *il*logical—this education did not prepare them for the practice of teaching music theatre voice, or for the increasing and acknowledged requirements to train other CCM styles within singing lessons.

Culture

Bourdieu argued that acquiring knowledge can become "a mechanism of social division".[28] Reflecting the individualised nature of habitus, the example of formal training and performance experience in classical voice provides insight into how the division of individual habitus worked. While some participants had highly successful classical performance experiences, others found that they did not fit the classical aesthetic. If a teacher's voice did not fit the aesthetic ideal of classical singing, they had difficulty finding performance work upon graduation. This resulted in separation and exclusion from the social world of classical music despite teachers' enculturation within this space through higher education.

One participant was a notable example of this separation from the cultural world of classical music which began while in graduate school. This participant was told by his graduate studies singing teacher that his voice was unsuitable for classical singing, and to expect to be excluded from his career before even starting. Apart from raising questions about why they were accepted to a classical performance programme, this situation was further complicated once they graduated and discovered that the training was *not* appropriate for musical theatre, or classical, or seemingly anything. They retrained themselves and managed to find a vocal production which allowed them access to a musical theatre career, without the help of voice teachers within academia. This teacher was not a cultural fit within the classical voice community and moved (or chose to move) out of the classical voice performance cultural group. They consequently discovered a sense of belonging in the musical theatre cultural group.

As an example of how individual histories can be experienced both on a personal level and within a social group, another participant described a similar experience of not fitting into either cultural group upon graduating from a classical voice degree:

> I went to New York ... to do some auditions where I was constantly met with, if I were singing for opera agents, um, they said "It's a very lovely voice, but it's not very operatic." And then somebody would take me to a musical theatre call in New York, and they would say "wow, you're obviously a very trained singer, but it sounds **so** operatic."[29]

For this participant, teaching musical theatre singing came at the price of separation from classical culture and social structures. This separation was made clear to them through their treatment by (classical) faculty colleagues—they were they excluded from social events and voice department meetings, despite being a member of the voice faculty.

Habitus informs the way members structure a field, and then position themselves within it. The participant teachers independently moved into the social space of musical theatre voice pedagogy from the space of classical voice performance, an action which was independently generated according to each teacher's experiences, background, embodied dispositions, and histories. Maton comments that "we learn ... our rightful place in the social world, where we will do best given our dispositions and resources, and also where we will struggle ... and ... try to avoid those fields that involve a field–habitus clash".[30] Participants moved towards a cultural group where they were less likely to experience the "social clash" they experienced within the classical voice performance cultural space.

Family background

In terms of family background, participants discussed how their musical learning was encouraged in their home life growing up, confirming that "a musical habitus depends on a musical upbringing".[31] A common familial background story involved early piano playing, encouragement of music lessons and performance experiences from a young age. Participants described singing in choirs. One participant commented "I've always sung, according to my mother I sang before I talked! Um, so, it was just something I did, I loved being in a choir and I was in children's musical theatre for years and years".[32] Another participant began piano lessons at age seven, commenting that "my stepmom made me practice". He played for church services at age 11 and sang and played for the school choir in junior high (7th to 9th grades). This teacher also played trumpet and French horn and was involved in a barbershop quartet and musical theatre in high school. Another teacher studied piano from grade two, yet another began piano lessons at age four. This teacher commented:

> I was singing from the get-go ... I was just involved in choirs in church and in school choirs. And then, my mother, being a proper southern lady believed that you had to have lessons to be

well rounded, so, um, I took voice lessons in high school and I also took drama lessons because that's what you did.[33]

While each individual teacher had specific and slightly different musical experiences at a young age, all were supported in their engagement with music by their family. Participants describe being enculturated into a societal norm of "proper southern" culture through both lessons, ("That's what you did") and music performance in church and choirs. Another teacher's description of being made to practice by their stepmother, even though "I fought her on it"[34] further symbolises the importance and value placed on music lessons and music performance within the family environment. Valuing music education was common in the family backgrounds of all interviewed participants, a sensibility embodied within every participant in the study. This sensibility influenced each participant's movement towards academic study of music and a career in the performing arts. This also points to a specific socioeconomic, class-based disposition and background. Taking music lessons and the support of children in music education and performance opportunities implies that there is both the time and the finances to support such activities in the family home.

Discussion: Habitus and musical theatre voice pedagogy

Education, culture, family background, ethnicity, gender, and time period intersect powerfully in relation to the habitus of the participant group. The teachers' backgrounds and dispositions, which emerged through the informal conversations and interviews, combined to suggest an enculturation into a classical music career, however, this group of teachers all had personal actions, decisions, and beliefs which propelled them individually away from classical voice performance and towards musical theatre voice pedagogy. While teachers displayed independence and agency—habitus is not necessarily deterministic—their collective career trajectory, dispositions, education, and backgrounds were largely (although not all the same) similar enough to be able to be identifiable as a specific cultural group, as outlined above. Importantly, however, as a group participants represented a point of differentiation—rather than reproducing their own voice pedagogical training and thereby reproducing their habitus in their own students, they exist in an "in-between" place, anomalies in the field who work in a space of ambiguity between their existing habitus and current practice.

Bourdieu acknowledges that individual agency means that a group will never be deterministic in action, and in this study individual agency was demonstrated through a movement *into* musical theatre away from classical voice performance and the habitus of upbringing and education. Here habitus both reflects how social structures are not "deterministic of behaviour"[35] but also how habitus creates its own cultural logics to establish fields. There is a collective, cultural logic as individual participants found their "fit" in the music theatre education space. This choice, this action to turn towards musical theatre singing and then, for some teachers, to move further towards CCM voice training, is reflective of the "social regularities with the experience of agency".[36] Individual participants displayed considerable agency. Those participants with classical training changed career trajectories by moving away from their classical background and training towards the cultural space of musical theatre for their own specific reasons and purposes. This in turn creates the "logic" that music theatre voice teachers within academia in the United States tend to have classical voice performance backgrounds.

The effects of habitus are embodied and deep. The physical display within studio teaching spaces of classical performance degree testamurs, combined with a background in classical voice performance was a significant area of ambiguity. Participants' background and training in classical voice performance created a pull in these teachers, between their habitus and their practice, which then created further tension in the positioning of music theatre voice teachers in relationship to the larger field of voice pedagogy. Earlier I discussed how participants practiced the teaching of musical theatre repertoire and, to a greater or lesser degree, adjusted their pedagogy to teach CCM styles. The prominent display of classical voice performance degrees in private studios may, however, powerfully signal to a musical theatre student that this teaching space is not open to them as a career option without classical voice performance credentials of their own. Further, teachers were critical and at times dismissive of their education in terms of preparing them for their pedagogical careers. Concomitantly, they discussed the joy of "singing above the stave" (a classical soprano), or the stimulation and joy of classical voice performance study:

Habitus and capitals of musical theatre singing teachers 99

"classical music for me was intellectually very stimulating. I liked that I was never bored. I was always challenged. I had to work very hard to do well".[37] Classical voice performance training and performance was not necessarily perceived as a negative part of the teacher's habitus; indeed, it was often a source of pride.

The positive perception of classical voice performance training for some participants might be based on the "position in the occupational class structure"[38] it bestowed upon them—it gave them an entry into the field of academic teaching of voice. The academic credentials displayed on the studio walls of teachers signals a "cultural competence"[39] to the academy, even when the field in which they are teaching requires different practices and skills (different cultural competences).[40] Here, the relation between habitus and practice is discordant, indicating a point of fracture within the voice pedagogy profession. Maton suggests that when "the field changes more rapidly than, or in different directions to, the habitus of its members the practices of social agents can then seem anachronistic, stubbornly resistant or ill-informed".[41]

Participant background in classical music was responsible for a tension between habitus and practice—participants were at once proud of their classical qualifications and experiences, while also acknowledging the inadequacies of their training in terms of their work within the musical theatre and CCM genres. Additionally, many teachers taught students classical voice function and style within lessons, while also acknowledging that they themselves needed to retrain their own voices out of classical voice style to understand the functional and stylistic differences between musical theatre singing and their own classical backgrounds. So, while teachers were at once rejecting the reproduction of their own educational habitus in classical music, some participants continued to teach classical function and style, perhaps for them to feel that their students had "legitimacy" in their training. In alignment with this classical background, in practice few teachers demonstrated specific skills teaching the intricacies of function and styles in the CCM repertoire currently dominant in the music theatre industry.

This tension between the educational habitus and current practice is significant in terms of the reproduction of practice within the field of music theatre voice pedagogy. If habitus is "the reproducer of structures",[42] this analysis of the data demonstrates that there is a curious tension within academia in the United States concerning the apparent privileging of a "legitimate" classical foundation over the distinct stylistic, aesthetic, and practical elements of musical theatre. This rendering of traditional, classical voice training approaches within the music theatre classroom, while aesthetically and stylistically inappropriate, nonetheless carried a certain prestige as the "legitimate" way to establish a career as a musical theatre teacher.

From habitus to capitals

In Bourdieu's works, habitus provides the foundation from which capitals emerge and find activation. A "well-formed habitus" involves enculturation into the dispositions of a specific group. This habitus confers a social advantage within the arbitrary rules of that particular cultural group. Habitus also frames understandings of the capitals at work within a social space and the modelling of behaviours within that specific space. For example, teachers who model professional behaviours, an implicit structure of the signature pedagogy of musical theatre voice teaching, indoctrinate the student into the profession through informing and developing the habitus required to enter the social space of a discipline.[43] Specifically, teachers pass on attitudes and dispositions appropriate to being a musical theatre performer through their own background as a performer via the one-to-one teaching modality. Further, knowledge of the need for idiosyncratic, tailored repertoire which values and promotes the individual performer's understanding of taste, or what Bourdieu identifies as "distinction", within the musical theatre discipline is one example of a well-formed habitus working *through* the capitals, signifying a student's arrival into the discipline of musical theatre and their position within this field.

Capitals and musical theatre voice teaching

Bourdieu's conception of the capitals extends the traditional idea of economic capital to other types of "assets" which are recognised as valuable within a specific cultural or social group. The type and value of a particular capital are seemingly arbitrary when viewed from outside a particular cultural group, but within the group feed into the logic of how a group is formed and what is considered valuable. The possession and trajectory of a particular capital plays an important role in determining an individual's position within a field, or social/cultural group, relative to other members of that group. Bourdieu often calls this arbitrary nature of capitals within a particular group a "misrecognition" of the value of a particular capital. This is notable because the significance of the specific capital may be only pertinent to a particular field; for instance, upon leaving the field and moving into another social group the same capital may be rendered of lower, or even inconsequential value. For example, within the social space of classical voice performance, an operatic soloist who has performed at, say, the Met in New York, or in Covent Garden in London has high "capital" within the cultural group of classical voice performers. However, while the same artist may be *respected* for their mastery and talent, they would not hold the same capital within, say, country music or in a performance at the Grand Ole Opry; in fact, the classical performer's capital would likely be low given that the operatic singer would not have the necessary capability to perform to the level of skill demanded by this specific genre of music in that specific space.

Bourdieu identified different types of "capitals" including "cultural capital", "social capital", and "symbolic capital", of which cultural and symbolic capital are particularly relevant to this study. Additionally, I observed and so have included "scientific capital"[44] in the discussion of the capitals displayed by the participant teachers encountered in this study.

Cultural capital

Cultural capitals are those capitals which are both inherited and acquired.[45] Inherited capitals involve absorbing cultural competences through the social environment in which an individual is raised. Inherited capital implies a certain way of living and being—for instance, how to decorate, what to eat, what is considered entertainment, and so on. The most powerful kind of acquired cultural capital is educational capital. Educational capital bestows a strong cultural capital on the bearer due to its legitimisation by an accredited institution. This kind of capital is itself subject to variation of valuation depending on the "speed of progress through the system"[46] and the type of educational qualification an individual gains.[47]

Specific types of cultural capital are used and embodied to strengthen the teacher's position within the field of musical theatre voice pedagogy, and to distinguish them from other individuals within the field of general voice pedagogy. These capitals are important to identify in order to construct the field, to examine how members within the specific field are positioned relative to one another, and to recognise what is considered an asset within that field.[48] Dominant among the cultural capitals voice teachers embody are the behaviours, relationships, social networking, and understandings they attain over time in the context of habitus as received through their education.

In terms of material forms of cultural capital, the display of items including past performance posters, large quantities of sheet music pertaining to musical theatre styles, theatre programmes of plays and musicals attended, pictures of past students and signed headshots of successful students are all ways in which teachers demonstrate and display their cultural capital within the studio space. Interestingly, while there was considerable display of musical theatre posters, sheet music, and so on, many participants also displayed/stored vast amounts of classical music sheet music in their private studio space, with these acting as symbolic reminders and visual cues of the training and background of teachers to both students and faculty who visit this space.

The performance of classical repertoire within musical theatre programmes, and the recognition of the "value" that classical voice education and background provides, functioned as marks of distinction within the observed musical theatre voice lessons. This value persisted despite teachers declaring the specific distinction of musical theatre performance style and function as being very different to classical voice singing styles. Many teachers also stored/displayed CCM style sheet music books on bookshelves, used as a resource within lessons and indicating specific depth of knowledge regarding the variety of repertoire required within the musical theatre discipline—another distinction of musical theatre voice pedagogy. While I did not observe teachers use amplification within the lessons, four teachers did have this equipment within their studios. In this way, the display of teachers' material cultural capital consisted of resources which looked back to the

Habitus and capitals of musical theatre singing teachers 103

past (classical performance degrees, sheet music, text books), that confirmed their skill and knowledge of their main activity of their teaching (musical theatre sheet music, texts, etc.), and turned towards the future (the addition of CCM style sheet music, amplification systems).

How teachers taught various styles also demonstrated an *embodied* form of cultural capital. The practice, dissemination, and embodiment of classical singing style (in addition to and comparative with musical theatre style and function) occurring within many of the studios indicates that these teachers value and hold on to the cultural capital bestowed on them through their training backgrounds, and that this is an important part of their habitus which is considered valuable and is to be passed on to their students. This ability to perform and teach classically endows a legitimacy to their teaching and, by extension, to the student in entering the discipline, whether or not they ever use these stylistic approaches to training in their professional lives. One teacher commented:

> I mean I've heard some seasoned musical theatre performers say "Oh, but I certainly do classical, I know that's the foundation of all of it" and that's how I hear these things, so I think there's still an undercurrent of that.[49]

However, not all teachers felt that students required classical function to be adequately trained as musical theatre performers. Only one teacher did not teach *any* classical style, repertoire, or function to students within lessons. Another teacher taught classical style and function, but no classical repertoire to students. A participant commented to me in a video catch up a year after my visit to their university that during my site visit, they had previously taught from a belief that "classical training is the foundation that takes you everywhere".[50] However, in the year that passed this teacher's opinion and practice underwent a dramatic transformation to the point that when we discussed classical voice training and practice for musical theatre students, their response was "it's frustrating because they don't need it".[51]

Beliefs regarding the value of classical training for musical theatre students, while still regarded as important by most of these teachers, are changing rapidly. This is indicative of a large shift occurring within the field of musical theatre voice pedagogy. Participants acknowledged that the teaching of CCM style and function to musical theatre students has become increasingly important for industry competitiveness. In conversations about the future of musical theatre voice pedagogy, some participants who currently have classical training within their syllabus acknowledged that the removal of classical voice repertoire requirements completely from musical theatre programmes may occur in the future within their programmes. The idea of classical training, repertoire, function, and style inclusion as an asset within the cultural capitals of musical theatre voice pedagogy—while still an acknowledged entrée into academic teaching—may be shifting in value within the field itself. The ability to competently teach pop, rock, and other CCM genres is becoming increasingly valuable within the musical theatre pedagogical sub-field. This may be a generational change—notably those participants who were over 55 were less likely to have engaged in further professional development into specific style and function of CCM pedagogy and were also more likely to have experienced specific challenges to their professional practice and the academic validity of musical theatre voice pedagogy within their academic careers.

The surface structures of musical theatre pedagogy included how teachers demonstrated a knowledge of repertoire and the ability to seek out under-performed repertoire while tailoring these songs to student attributes, the ability to discern and teach speech quality, the training of specific musical theatre style and function (for example, belt) and the importance of acting and dance, and synthesis of skills. These attributes and skills are significant in how this specific embodied knowledge becomes a cultural capital in the field of musical theatre voice pedagogy. This specialised knowledge (realised through practice) distinguishes musical theatre voice teachers within the general field of voice teachers. These skills and knowledges are valued highly within the musical theatre voice pedagogy field and carry a high cultural capital in this sub-field within voice pedagogy. They are operationalised as a marker of taste, or distinction within the field from other types of singing teaching.

Educational capital

Embodied cultural capital and material cultural capital are assets which contribute to overall amounts of cultural capital, and the volume of cultural capital an individual possesses is significantly boosted by the legitimacy endowed to teachers through their predominantly classical music educational qualifications. All teachers held a master's degree at a minimum, and some held doctoral degrees, with these educational credentials providing valuable assets—without these qualifications teachers cannot access academic teaching opportunities. These credentials are an "institutionalised form of capital"[52] which are produced by, and certified through, universities. Higher education certifies that a person has a level of "cultural competence",[53] and a person without a qualification, who has "uncertified cultural capital ... (will) always be required to prove themselves, because they are only what they do".[54] If education certifies the holder of the qualification and gives access to a field, here it is clear that because the certifications displayed were largely in classical voice performance this has a large asset value within the cultural capital of music theatre voice pedagogy in the context of this study. Further, teachers who "are only what they do", but who may be experts in the field of musical theatre or other CCM genres are therefore excluded from the academic teaching field because they often do not have the accepted type of educational capital required to enter this arena.

When considering educational qualifications, different degrees have distinctive asset values depending on the specific certifying institution. Universities themselves are in competition with each other for academic capital because "the education system is a hidden system of inequalities".[55] This system of inequality is evident in the ways universities have various ranking systems. Websites such as topuniversities.com, timeshighereducation.com, and gooduniversitiesguide.com all offer rankings of universities based on various criteria. In the United States, Ivy League Universities, or universities with particularly high reputations for music and musical theatre compared to small, lesser-known state and private schools have different amounts of educational capital and therefore bestow different amounts of cultural capital on the individual within the cultural group of music teachers.

Within the social space of voice teachers, this may be fractured into ever smaller groups of institutions which specialise in classical styles, institutions which have a high educational capital for musical theatre (as determined by the success of alumni from these programmes in successfully gaining employment within the industry), and the considerably smaller numbers of institutions which produce CCM specialists. While contentious and highly subjective, universities use such rankings to boost their educational capital in the academic marketplace. Interestingly, I noted many of the participant teachers had attended some of these (subjectively) highly ranked schools within the music discipline—thereby reproducing the value of their alma maters in their ability to bestow academic credibility though employment within academia. In addition, the networking gained through educational experiences provides a boost to the social capital an individual possesses. This social capital proves especially valuable within the larger field of voice pedagogy when looking for academic employment, as these social networks can provide references which increase legitimacy to a teacher's suitability both in skill level and dispositions (habitus).

The perception of the relative values of educational capital and the need for a high educational capital as an asset within the field of voice pedagogy might explain the tension between teachers using and displaying their classical voice performance degrees (high educational capital) despite acknowledging these degrees were not necessarily useful for producing the kinds of styles they required to teach musical theatre voice (practice). In *Distinction*, Bourdieu[56] discusses the higher status and position of those familiar with classical music in the social hierarchy. Despite the decades passed, and despite the emergence of contemporary music, jazz, and musical theatre degrees, classical music still holds significant asset value within academia.[57]

Scientific capital

Scientific capital is measured as an asset and materialises through science-based textbooks and measurement-taking instruments. It privileges "rationality", through knowledge of the problem field, and through the ability to solve problems using "objectivity",[58] if objectivity is even possible. The selection of measuring an action or quality of singing itself is a subjective choice by the researcher. In the field of voice pedagogy scientific capital is both a cultural capital—it must be acquired and certified through the educational certification process—and a symbolic capital. There has been a pedagogical movement towards functional voice teaching and evidence-based practice for voice teaching.[59] This type of voice training is based on combining known voice science (physiology and acoustic information), teaching considerations of style, teacher expertise and experience, and student goals in the practice of voice teaching. Basic voice science is considered an asset and valued as a type of capital within the voice pedagogy community. Short courses in voice science and acoustics for singing have emerged in recent years. These courses, often run during the summer break, confer legitimised, certified knowledge in this field. Further promoting the use of science in voice teaching, and therefore elevating its importance in the field of voice pedagogy, the National Association of Teachers of Singing (NATS) provide a free online resource, www.vocapedia.info, for voice teachers to have access to relevant areas of voice science.

Singing voice teachers who have knowledge of voice science and understand the implications scientific findings may have on the singing voice are holders of scientific capital within the larger voice pedagogy community when compared with those who have limited, or no scientific knowledge. Membership of cross-disciplinary bodies (made up of voice scientists and researchers, laryngologists and medical researchers, speech language pathologists, and singing teachers), publication within their journals, and attendance and presentations at conferences affords singing teachers increased scientific capital within the field of voice pedagogy. Certification in short courses on voice science provides credibility to teachers who gain professional development in a legitimised way, as opposed to those who study and learn voice science independently who have no legitimised way of "proving" what they know. Cross-disciplinary research is encouraged by NATS, through awards such as The Van Lawrence Award, and regular columns within its journal focused on voice science.

Research participants demonstrated scientific capital through the display of anatomical posters on the wall and the display/storage of voice science and vocology textbooks on bookshelves. Additionally, the use of voice science knowledge within lessons and explanation of function to explain and explore vocal choices were ways in which this capital was used in practice. However, while voice teachers with a high level of scientific knowledge command high amounts of scientific capital, one participant, who possessed high levels of this capital, questioned the value to the *practice* and art of singing teaching:

> we also have the researcher voice teacher, who, that doesn't really work out either if they've never performed onstage. They don't know what's required of a singer.[60]

This participant felt strongly that teaching required research, teaching, *and* performance skills to understand all aspects of singing voice teaching. Only a few participants considered themselves researchers or voice science experts despite most teachers displaying applied practice of voice acoustics, physiology, and other "science-based" knowledge in lessons.

In my study these teachers often displayed intuitive scientific knowledge in their practice but did not consider themselves educated in voice science (lower scientific capital). I observed these participants defer to colleagues with *certified* educational capital within voice science as being more expert in the field. As one participant noted in terms of how they negotiate questions related to voice science: "I send them to BG",[61] another teacher on faculty with certified voice science credentials. This referral process occurred despite the teacher often displaying other considerable strengths in their practice, including an intuitive understanding of scientific principles of acoustics and physiology.

Symbolic capital

Symbolic capital includes those dispositions, or characteristics or which are (mis)recognised by a field as having an arbitrary value in and of themselves within a field. It is the *unquestioned* nature of the symbolic capital that gives it a kind of logic within the field of practice—it is just "the way things are"—and what Bourdieu contends makes symbolic capital a *mis*recognised asset.

In the field of musical theatre voice pedagogy, as demonstrated by my participants' backgrounds, symbolic capital is granted to individuals with a strong performance background. Those teachers who have performed on Broadway, or in National Tours are considered to have a higher symbolic value in the academic field of teaching than teachers with performance experience outside of these spheres. This powerful asset holds high academic value regardless of teaching skill and training of the individual. Mastery of singing technique, and successful employment as demonstrated by a successful Broadway or National touring company career, is automatically translated into an asset of high symbolic capital within the voice pedagogy community. For example, one participant held doctoral-level specialisation in pedagogy, and when I asked about advertisements for jobs asking for performers with Broadway or national profiles, they commented that their lack of experience in this area was "the thing that holds me back from getting those jobs".[62] Yet another participant commented that leaving a doctoral programme to work in New York meant that "my professional track was more marketable than what my degree track was at that time".[63]

The type and location of performance in musical theatre determines the symbolic value of the teacher in the field in terms of accessing academic employment. As demonstrated by the following example, performance skills have historically been considered more valuable than teaching skills in music education in academia. Further, classical voice performance as the standard of "safety" for singing were outlined by one participant:

> DGG, the one woman that taught musical theatre when I was a student here, was head of the division. She called me and at the time I had been doing both, ... classical rep, [and] musical theatre rep, and she said "we're looking for somebody to teach the musical theatre kids" and she wanted at the time someone with a classical background, which she thought as "healthy singing" who was also *performing* musical theatre rep, and so she said "I think you would be the perfect person to do that because you do have feet in both camps". So, I said, "OK", believe it or not, I never taught a practice lesson, for anybody to see me.[64]

While this teacher at the time of my visit was clearly a successful teacher who, it should be noted, discussed in detail the pedagogical training pursued over the course of their teaching career—and I stress that I am not questioning the skill of the participant— this excerpt demonstrates the institutionalised symbolic capital accorded to those who can perform musical theatre repertoire in *addition* to classical repertoire. Further, this excerpt illustrates how musical theatre performance credits were historically not considered *as* legitimate as the combination of classical and musical theatre. This example also highlights the institutional bias against musical theatre voice technique as vocally dangerous and classical voice style as safe and the standard required for academic appointment.

It is unthinkable that teachers in other spheres of pedagogy (for example, high school or primary school teachers) be allowed to practice without any form of teacher training and accompanying state-based or national accrediting registrational body. Indeed, a teacher who understands how to translate required artistic skills in practice using pedagogical skill is more valued by students than an expert performer with no teaching skills.[65] However, the symbolic capital afforded to those with performance careers permeates the field of voice pedagogy within academia.

There is long held assumption in HME that those who can *do*, can *teach*.[66] This is often the case in higher education generally, where teaching qualifications have traditionally been secondary to mastery of disciplinary knowledge, esteem, and standing within a specific discipline. In the specific case of musical theatre voice pedagogy, this is further represented by the cultural capital of voice performance bachelor, master's, and doctoral degrees which focus on vocal performance. AT commented about singing teaching as a profession:

AT: *(Quoting from the Internet)* "A profession is a paid occupation that involves prolonged training and formal qualification" ... there *has* to be some sort of *standard*. And we don't have a standard. There are people teaching right now who know nothing about voice teaching. They are still able to do it. Dog grooming has more standards than we have. *(Researcher laughs)*. You have to be licensed to groom a dog. Because in general, you know, a society licenses people that can harm something. We still haven't even got to that level where people understand that we can harm someone. I mean, we *(signals R and AT)* know that ...
R: Yeah
AT: ... but not everyone knows that, um, that required formalised education. Formalised education in what? I

Habitus and capitals of musical theatre singing teachers 111

mean, there are people that are teaching voice that had to do three recitals and that's all they did. They didn't even take the pedagogy class. And yet their profession is voice teaching. Their profession is **not** singing! It's voice teaching. That's what they do on a daily basis.[67]

Within the space of musical theatre voice pedagogy in academia, the preferment of teachers' performance background over formal teaching credentials is an example of the Bourdieu's concept of misrecognition. This is symbolic capital, where an "asset" central to this capital aligns more closely with disciplinary mastery than the pedagogical skill required in the day-to-day practice of teaching.

The symbolic capital afforded by a performance career provides the bearer of this background with a significant asset within the field of musical theatre voice teaching. While educational capital—in the form of the appropriate qualification—acts as a gatekeeper for determining entry into the academic teaching realm, a performance career with both National or Broadway experience may extend this asset, and in some cases be exchanged for academic appointment. Indeed, the possession by a teacher of this kind of performance experience can enhance the status of university and be a highly valued recruitment tool. Universities which require significant performance experience may overlook a lack of teaching experience or training, as the potential teacher with a national performance profile carries a caché which misrecognises the value of the asset (to both the university and potential students) and overrides teaching skill and qualifications.[68]

Social capital

Within the field of voice pedagogy social capital is made up of the networks between professionals and the recognition and status given to members of the field. Social capital is a commodity which may be useful in ensuing employment at the academic level, as one job advertisement demonstrates by requesting that the applicant "maintain a high level of professional visibility and leadership in the field".[69] These networks are established in a number of ways. Firstly, social capital is gained through educational connection. An individual who can attest to a social knowledge of another teacher by way of attending the same undergraduate or graduate programme will hold social capital through the recognition of each other in the field. This recognition creates a baseline of social capital. This capital may then be increased through an increase of cultural capital—for example, when the graduate experience was at a highly ranked university.

Secondly, social capital is also gained through employment connections. Those who are employed at the same university carry social capital through connections with each other. The social capital is then used and recognised at events organised by professional networking organisations, for example, conferences run by NATS, or The Voice Foundation. Those members of these organisations who hold office possess additional social capital which is used and recognised at these events through their visibility in the running of conferences.

Thirdly, social capital may be employed in the use of references for employment. Having references from those in the field who have high social capital can bestow additional social capital on the applicant. If the candidate is then successful, the candidate's social capital increases through the new employment network. The existing high social capital of the candidate, through association, also increases the social capital of those employed at the institution, and the institution itself.

The particular types of capitals outlined above are those which were present in the context of this study, and while they may not be universalised across the entire field of voice pedagogy, are presented in the spirit of Bourdieu's concept of a "particular case of the possible".[70] This chapter has outlined the habitus and capitals displayed by participants in this study. While I have here identified habitus and capital as separate entities, it must be noted that this is an artificial separation, and when using Bourdieu's theoretical concepts, it is through the relationship and interaction of habitus and the capitals within a field that **practice** is enacted. This is important to note, because it was an investigation into the practices, training, and background of musical theatre voice teachers that guided this study.

Notes

1 Grenfell, 2008, p. 44.
2 Ibid., p. 46.

3 Bourdieu, 1979/2010, p. 468.
4 Ibid., p. 95.
5 Maton, 2008.
6 Ibid., p. 51.
7 Power, 1999, p. 49.
8 I understand that there are more specific and varied gender identifiers and in this study I have at times during this thesis used "they theirs" to de-identify the gender of participants where I felt appropriate. Gender identity was not a specific focus of the study.
9 Smith, 2015.
10 Ibid., p. 70.
11 National Centre for Educational Statistics, 2019.
12 Sergeant and Himonides, 2022.
13 www.zippia.com/voice-teacher-jobs/demographics/
14 Overland, 2016.
15 Ibid.
16 Brower & James, 2020; Frank, 2020; Gamage et al., 2020; Gardiner et al., 2007; Hult et al., 2005; Kjeldal et al., 2005; Mansfield et al., 2019.
17 For a fascinating discussion on the ways in which academic work is gendered, see Kjeldal et al. (2005). For an account of the ways in which men benefit from sexually harassing women in academia, see Mansfield et al. (2019).
18 National Centre for Education Statistics, 2019.
19 The Asian American Actors Coalition, 2017.
20 National Association of Schools of Music, 2020.
21 Bronstein, 2019, para. 4.
22 Feder & McGill, 2021.
23 Kajikawa, 2019.
24 Some teachers may have been of an age where they could have studied at Penn State's Masters in Musical Theatre Voice Pedagogy program, however the design of the program is limited to one enrolment at a time (Turnbow et al., 2014). This is an unusual structure for a voice pedagogy program, which are usually taught in larger cohort sizes.
25 Interview transcription, University M.
26 Interview transcription, University T.
27 Kajikawa, 2019.
28 Robbins, 2008, p. 33.
29 Interview transcription, University G.
30 Maton, 2008, pp. 58–59.
31 Söderman et al., 2015, p. 9.
32 Interview transcription, University M.
33 Interview transcription, University V.
34 Interview transcription, University Q.
35 Power, 1999, p. 48.
36 Maton, 2008, p. 55.

37 Interview transcription, University M.
38 Bennett, 2010, p. xix.
39 Bourdieu, 1979/2010, p. xxv.
40 It should be noted that some skills gained in a classical music degree would certainly translate to musical theatre voice teaching, and participants demonstrated these skills. In particular, participants demonstrated music theory, music history, aural, and music reading skills during observed lessons. However, participants did not *comment* on these competencies being useful to them, rather that they required additional training outside of their classical training to gain competency in teaching musical theatre singing.
41 Maton, 2008, p. 59.
42 Power, 1999, p. 49.
43 For more detailed reporting of the deep, implicit, and surface structures see Cox (2020).
44 Moore, 2008.
45 Bourdieu, 1979/2010.
46 Ibid., p. 75.
47 Söderman et al., 2015.
48 Bourdieu & Wacquant, 1992; Power, 1999.
49 Interview transcription, University X.
50 Reflexive journal entry, April 2020.
51 Reflexive journal entry, April 2020.
52 Moore, 2008, p. 106.
53 Bourdieu, 1979/2010, p. xxv.
54 Ibid., p. 15.
55 Söderman et al., 2015, p. 8.
56 Bourdieu, 1979/2010.
57 Kajikawa, 2019.
58 Moore, 2008, p. 106.
59 Benson, 2018; LeBorgne & Rosenberg, 2014; LoVetri, 2013; Ragan, 2018.
60 Interview transcription, University T.
61 Interview transcription, University G.
62 Interview transcription, University T.
63 Interview transcription, University V.
64 Interview transcription, University G.
65 Watling et al., 2013.
66 Persson, 1996.
67 Interview transcription, University T.
68 I would note that the connections and enculturation of social disposition a performer who transfers to teaching may bring to the teaching room may be of considerable importance to the student experience

and employment outcomes. It is just that the student may not receive the same pedagogical skill from a teacher lacking pedagogical training.
69 Florida State University, 2020.
70 Bourdieu, 1979/2010, p. xiii.

References

Bennett, T. (2010). Introduction to the Routledge Classics Edition. In P. Bourdieu, *Distinction: A social critique of the judgement of taste* (R. Nice, Trans) (pp. xvii–xxiii). Routledge. (Original work published 1979).

Benson, E. (2018). Modern voice pedagogy: Functional training for all styles. *American Music Teacher*, *67*(6), 10–13.

Bourdieu, P. (2010). *Distinction: A social critique of the judgement of taste* (R. Nice, Trans). Routledge. (Original work published 1979).

Bourdieu P., & Wacquant, L. (1992). *An invitation to reflexive sociology*. Polity.

Bronstein, P. (2019, June 24). Diversity will save classical music and it starts with music education. *Insight into Diversity*. www.insightintodiversity.com/diversity-will-save-classical-music-and-it-starts-with-music-education/

Brower A., & James, A. (2020) Research performance and age explain less than half of the gender pay gap in New Zealand universities. *PLoS ONE*, *15*(1), e0226392. doi: 10.1371/journal.pone.0226392

Cox, D. 2020. *In the room where it happens: teaching musical theatre and Contemporary Commercial Music (CCM) singing*. Doctoral Thesis. USQ E-prints. https://eprints.usq.edu.au/40200/7/DCOX%20THESIS%20FINAL.pdf

Feder, S., & McGill, A. (2021). Diversity, equity, inclusion, and racial injustice in the classical music professions: A call to action. In M. Beckerman & P Boghossian (Eds.), *Classical music: Contemporary perspectives and challenges* (pp. 87–102). Open Book Publishers.

Frank, J. (2020). The persistence of the gender pay gap in British Universities. *Fiscal Studies*, *41*(4), 889–903.

Gamage, D., Kavetsos, G., Mallick, S., & Sevilla, A., (2020). *Pay transparency initiative and gender pay gap: Evidence from research-intensive universities in the UK*. IZA Institute of Labour Economics. https://docs.iza.org/dp13635.pdf

Gardiner, M., Tiggemann, M., Kearns, H., & Marshall, K., (2007). Show me the money! An empirical analysis of mentoring outcomes for women in academia. *Higher Education and Research Development*, *26*(4), 425–442. doi: 10.1080/07294360701658633

Grenfell, M. (2008). Part II: Field theory: Beyond subjectivity and objectivity. Introduction. In M. Grenfell (Ed.), *Pierre Bourdieu: Key concepts* (pp. 43–48). Acumen.

Hult, C., Callister, R., & Sullivan, K. (2005). Is there a global warming toward women in academia. *Liberal Education*, Summer / Fall, 50–57.

Kajikawa, L. (2019). The possessive investment in classical music: Confronting legacies of white supremacy in U.S. schools and departments of music. In K. W Krenshaw, L. C. Harris, D.M Hosang, & G. Lipsitz (Eds.), *Seeing race again* (1st edition, pp. 155–174). University of California Press. doi: 10.1525/9780520972148-008

Kjeldal, S., Rindfleish, J., & Sheridan, A., (2005). Deal making and rule breaking: Behind the façade of equity in academia. *Gender and Education*, *17*(4), 431–437. doi: 10.1080/09540250500145130

LeBorgne, W., & Rosenberg, M. D. (2014). *The vocal athlete*. Plural.

LoVetri, J. (2013). The necessity of using functional training in the independent studio. *Journal of Singing*, *70*(1), 79–86.

Mansfield, B., Lave, R., McSweeney, K., Bonds, A., Cockburn, J., Domosh, M., Hamilton, T., Hawkins, R., Hessl, A., Munroe, D., Ojeda, D., & Radel, C. (2019). It's time to benefit how men's career's benefit from sexually harassing women in academia. *Human Geography*, *12*(1), 82–87.

Maton, K. (2008). Habitus. In M. Grenfell (Ed.), *Pierre Bourdieu: Key concepts* (pp. 49–66). Acumen.

Moore, R. (2008). Capital. In M. Grenfell (Ed.), *Pierre Bourdieu: Key concepts* (pp. 101–118). Acumen.

National Association of Schools of Music (January 21, 2020). *National Association of Schools of Music handbook*. https://nasm.arts-accredit.org/wp-content/uploads/sites/2/2020/01/M-2019-20-Handbook-02-13-2020.pdf

National Centre for Education Statistics. (2019). *Race/ethnicity of college faculty*. https://nces.ed.gov/fastfacts/display.asp?id=61

Overland, C. (2016). Gender composition and salary of the music faculty in NASM Accredited universities: 2000–2014. *College Music Symposium: Exploring Diverse Perspectives*. doi: 10.18177/sym.2016.56.sr.11129

Persson, R. (1996). Studying with a musical maestro: A case study of commonsense teaching in artistic training. *Creativity Research Journal*, *9*(1), 33–46.

Power, E. (1999). An introduction to Pierre Bourdieu's key theoretical concepts. *Journal for the Study of Food and Society*, *3*(1), 48–52. doi: 10.2752/152897999786690753

Ragan, K. (2018). Defining evidence-based pedagogy: A new framework. *Journal of Singing*, *75*(2), 157–160.

Robbins, D. (2008). Theory of practice. In M. Grenfell (Ed.), *Pierre Bourdieu: Key concepts* (pp. 27–40). Acumen.

Sergeant, D., & Himonides, E. (2022). Performing sex: The representation of male and female musicians in three performance genres. *Psychology of Music*, 1–38. doi: 10.1177/03057356221115458

Smith, G. (2015). Masculine domination in private-sector popular music performance education in England. In P. Bunard, Y. Trulsson, & J. Söderman (Eds.), *Bourdieu and the sociology of music education* (pp. 61–78). Ashgate.

Söderman, J. Burnard, P. & Hofvander-Trulsson, Y. (2015). Contextualising Bourdieu in the field of music and music education. In Burnard, P., Trulsson, Y., & Söderman, J. (Eds.), *Bourdieu and the sociology of music education* (pp. 1–11). Ashgate.

The Asian American Actors Coalition. (2017). *Ethnic representation on New York stages*. www.aapacnyc.org/uploads/1/1/9/4/11949532/aapac_2016-2017_report.pdf

Turnbow, C., Saunders-Barton, M., & Spivey, N. (2014). Training the next generation of music theater voice teachers: Penn State's first MFA pedagogy grad takes stock. *Journal of Singing*, *71*(2), 217–220.

Watling, C., Driessen, E., van der Vleuten, C., Vanstone, M., & Lingard, L. (2013). Music lessons: Revealing medicine's learning culture through a comparison with that of music. *Medical Education*, *47*, 842–850.

7 The field of voice pedagogy

Field

Bourdieu describes the concept of field as "a network, or a configuration of objective relations between positions".[1] A field is a relational, structured, autonomous social space, likened to a field where a football game is played, containing boundaries and positions with specific rules which must be learned in order to participate.[2] Fields are competitive spaces, with boundaries determined by an internal logic based upon values identified through habitus and enacted through the capitals. Habitus determines a participant's position and power within a field, relative to other members, as represented through the possession, display, and trajectory of assets, or capitals, they possess. Bourdieu's conception of field is not that of an *even* playing field—the value and trajectory of capitals members possess will advantage, disadvantage, or equalise them relative to each other both upon entry to the field and during participation in "the game". Players in the field, by participating in the game, acknowledge the social or cultural group as a field and therefore the existence of a game in play. Participants, or members of the social group, make distinctions between their own capitals and "classify and qualify"[3] other members and themselves, situating themselves within the field according to where they determine they fit. This participation in the game of culture may occur below the level of consciousness, but it is through participation that the field is structured, constructed and through which the rules of the game are determined. Further, fields are autonomous, and have boundaries which, like force fields, which dissipate in strength once outside of them. Fields contain a whole "world" system of

DOI: 10.4324/9781003332572-7

hierarchies within them, with their own values, logics, and "ways things are done". This system can be seen clearly by those within the field but is often invisible to those outside of the field.

Musical theatre voice pedagogy is a sub-field, or specialisation, within the larger field of general voice pedagogy. Within the field of musical theatre voice pedagogy are members with various amounts of capitals and habitus who structure themselves in relation to each other. This structuring occurs through differentiation of their practices, capitals, and habitus, in relation to both each other and to other classical, musical theatre, and CCM voice teachers. Those teachers who have the highest positions within the field of musical theatre voice pedagogy within academia are those who have a combination of terminal degrees in classical voice performance (educational capital), have performed professionally on Broadway or in a national tour of a Broadway production (symbolic capital), and who have published (higher value) or presented (lower value) at voice teaching conferences (social capital) or at voice science conferences (scientific capital). This was supported in the study through teachers who, although they may hold an equivalent academic position, deferred to those colleagues with greater scientific capital, particularly if these colleagues had published their work. Further evidence of the way in which capitals work include the participant unable to access positions at certain "higher ranked" programmes due to a lack of symbolic capital represented by national tour or Broadway performance experience—this lack of a certain *type* of performance credential reduced their symbolic capital. Further dominance in the field is attributed to those who work in highly ranked musical theatre programmes and have a track record of teaching successful students in the industry (educational/cultural capital). Universities typically use this field dominance by promoting their successful alumni on websites to attract students as a display of faculty expertise and programme success.

Within the larger field of voice pedagogy there is a traditional hierarchy within the field, easily observed at any conference of voice teachers, and, by expansion, any conference of cross-disciplinary voice professionals. At the top of the field in positions of power are those (often classical) voice teachers who run professional organisations and who also generally hold university positions. Professional organisation executive membership creates considerable cultural and social capital, feeds into educational capital, and reinforces the power of educational capital within the field when these positions are held by university-based teachers. A recent job advertisement stated: "Priority will be given to candidates with a record of leadership in the National Association of Teachers of Singing (NATS)".[4] What this "record of leadership" brings is considerable cultural and social (networking) capital, which contributes to increasing the educational capital of the educational institution.

Similarly, voice science researchers who have university-based positions are often found in high-ranking executive positions within professional voice organisations. Professional organisations are sub-fields within the larger field of voice pedagogy and compete for prestige within this space, often having membership who consist of the same voice teachers, although some organisations may have an emphasis on science or cross-disciplinary approaches, while others are more focused on voice pedagogy and the artistry of performance. Many voice teachers and singing researchers who are based in institutions play the game of voice pedagogy through presenting at conferences, publishing in journals, and by holding executive positions within professional organisations. This is often a requirement for the teachers of gaining tenure in the US academic system.

These pedagogues in official positions in organisations hold considerable power about what is included and what is excluded or marginalised within the field through the selection of conference/journal contents and topics of study. What is considered "important" is what is chosen for research, selected as a presentation topic at a conference, and selected to be published in journals. The topics of research are given validation through this selection process, thereby reproducing the field. Through these processes scientific capital feeds into what is considered important knowledge within the field and therefore reinforces what is selected to be taught within educational institutions, and what is excluded.

The bulk of singing voice research has traditionally been focused on classically trained singers. This is most often conducted by those in academic positions which provide resources to support these research endeavours. Because highly placed individuals within professional organisations often come from the academic sector, the research that is conducted reinforces the biases of their particular interests, backgrounds, and training.

Positional power is exhibited where members of professional organisations congregate—for example, at conferences, through academic publications, and in online forums. These congregations of members form part of the exclusionary practices in the larger field of voice pedagogy. Hierarchies are maintained within these organisations because attendance and participation within these arenas increases capitals and positions members within the hierarchy in higher power positions. In this way, these professional organisations, their conferences, journals, and online forums are both structured and structuring. Access to publications is also often withheld for those who have no membership or access to university journal databases. In this way, those with educational and scientific capital continue to be able to increase this capital within the field and reproduce their own dominance. This often benefits those in more senior positions who are statistically (and historically) more likely to be white men.[5]

Participant teachers often structured themselves in the field by deferring to colleagues with greater certification in scientific knowledge about the singing voice. Expanding this observation, this hierarchical structure is reinforced within the larger voice pedagogy community. In the field of voice pedagogy, voice science researchers hold higher educational capital and therefore hold higher positions within the field than singing voice teachers without this capital. At a particular cross-disciplinary conference, this ranking is implied through the way in which the "cross-disciplinary" programme is ordered. Voice science presentations are delivered first, followed by medical sessions, then speech pathology sessions, and singing voice pedagogy sessions are held on the final day. In a clear indication of the lack of cross-disciplinary interaction, as the sessions progress, presentation rooms get smaller and smaller. While many voice teachers sit in on voice science, speech pathology, and medical research sessions, the same could not be said of many voice scientists and medical professionals observing singing voice teacher presentations. Within the voice community, this conference structure reinforces the implication that singing teachers were the least important presenters in attendance. Perhaps a different arrangement, where presentations of all disciplines were mixed in together might provide a more accurate representation of the inter-disciplinary approach promoted by the organisation.

Within the field of voice pedagogy, positions of power are asserted by those who have classical voice performance experience, classical voice performance educators, and those who teach highly accomplished professional students. Musical theatre teachers who possess scientific capital also assert higher positions in the cultural game in the sub-field of musical theatre voice pedagogy. Research participants openly discussed their experiences of going to conferences and feeling alienated by classical colleagues. One participant acknowledged the lower position of musical theatre voice teachers in the world of voice pedagogy, expressing frustration at going to conferences and having classical teachers comment after a music theatre masterclass that "belt singing is dangerous". That a classical teacher with no experience or training in musical theatre specialisation felt comfortable to proffer their opinion, and that these arguments still exist within voice pedagogy was offensive to this participant. It is also indicative of the classical teacher's lack of awareness of their own ignorance and demonstrative of the perceived superiority of classical teachers to speak up about a topic for which they have no expertise or experience. The opposite is unthinkable. I very much doubt that a musical theatre and CCM teacher would be courageous enough to voice an opinion about a classical singer's performance being "vocally dangerous" in a public forum such as a voice conference. CCM and musical theatre voice teachers understand what it is to "keep to their places" in such arenas.

Doxa and symbolic power

While Shulman's[6] concepts of signature pedagogies are useful to outline the structures and practices of a pedagogy, the use of Bourdieu's concepts here provides a framework to understand *how* and *why* certain practices constitute the social and professional activities within voice pedagogy. Doxa, in Bourdieu's work, refers to pre-reflexive, intuitive, and unquestioned beliefs based on knowledges, perceptions, and assumptions which are taken for granted.[7] In social and cultural groups doxa accounts for the meeting of actions and practice with mental and social structures which are unquestioned, misrecognised as symbolically important and therefore "reproduced in a self-reinforcing manner".[8] Doxa works when those who are playing the "cultural game" in the field do not question the legitimacy of the field or those who exert power within the field. Those in powerful positions use their existing capitals to reproduce the field and increase capitals, and therefore power, within a field. Doxa reflects the practices, attitudes, and ways of being within a field that are "the way things have always been done", taken for granted, and so go unquestioned.

Doxa is closely related to symbolic power within a field and is legitimised through the "language and linguistic exchanges and the misrecognised arbitrary classifications, categorisation and differentiation"[9] present and reproduced within a field. In the field of voice pedagogy, language and linguistic devices are used to exclude and marginalise genres other than classical singing. This exclusion has meant being kept distant from the power and reproductive sources, in particular the educational culture, of the field. Despite the attempt at legitimisation of CCM singing by the American Academy of Teachers of Singing,[10] CCM voice pedagogy remains under-represented in university programmes across the United States. The dominance of classical training within universities continues to reproduce teachers based on the classical model.

Extending this issue, within academia, advertisements for employment opportunities for voice teacher positions often assume a classical teacher is required—employment opportunities for singing voice teachers who are musical theatre or CCM specialists will generally explicitly state "musical theatre" or "contemporary" teacher in the job title. Employment opportunities for classical voice teachers will generally advertise for an "Assistant (or Associate) Professor of Voice" with the assumption that a professor of voice is a classical voice teacher. Linguistic cues serve to exclude those from the field without the required qualification, while providing an access point to those "in the know"—those who can decipher the linguistic code at work. The code indicating that a position is actually for a classically trained singing teacher includes statements such as "language skills for performing in English, Italian, German, and French", the ability to teach "courses in lyric diction", "direct the annual opera workshop", and a performance background "with a strong emphasis on classical music and opera". This language instantly sends the message to musical theatre and CCM voice specialists that these job positions are not available to them, despite the jobs being advertised as a "Professor of Voice".

These advertisements are speaking to specific candidates, in a specific way, while excluding candidates who are not "classical"—no CCM voice teacher would teach diction, French, Italian, or German within their daily practice (unless, perhaps, they happened to be working within French, Italian, or German popular music). These linguistic cues serve as gatekeepers to entry into the academic community, and refer to the ongoing reproduction of the field. Many jobs ask for teachers who teach classical *and* musical theatre styles, effectively cutting out musical theatre and CCM voice specialists without classical voice training from applying for these positions, and thus reproducing the field's status quo.

Ways in which this exclusion is used but not recognised by the classical voice community are present not only through the job application process where language cues articulate the classical dominance of the field. One participant tearfully recalled the following painful examples of social isolation and exclusion they experienced within the work environment which followed being asked to represent the university at an overseas singing competition for both musical theatre and classical voice styles (the teacher had a background in performance and qualifications of opera and a long musical theatre career):

AG: As a part of my faculty here, as I've said previously, very much an orphan. Um, very much not a part of the voice faculty, even in social situations ... When I was first asked to do the (overseas) trip, I contacted the head of voice who never responded, and never responded, and never responded. Um, I then just went to MGG, who you met in the elevator ... who is **her** (Head of Voice) boss. And I said "I've been offered this opportunity, um, this is paid for, this is paid for, it's primarily, ah, recruiting for the university ... And, um, the only thing that I have to ask from you is, is there money to fly me there?" And he said, "Oh, we have the, um, what's it called, The G Fund, this is a fund set up for only the voice division where they can bring in guest artists, they can do this and this." And he said "Yeah, we can take money out of that fund. It's for the Voice Faculty" and I said "OK". So, even though I'd written to the head of voice numerous times and not

	got a response, we run into each other in the ladies' room after MGG has already OK'd this.
R:	Yes?
AG:	And I said, "Happy to finally see you. This happened, and this and this and this." And I said, "So they want me to judge classical and musical theatre." She whipped her head around and she said, "You can't judge classical singing." And then she said, "You can't take that money from The G Fund, that's for the Voice Faculty." ... I said, "Excuse me, I am part of the Voice Faculty."
R:	Yeah ...
AG:	And she said "Oh, we're going to have to talk about this." And then MGG said, "I don't care what she says, you can have that money." So, I said, here's the thing, that's the culmination of 23 years here. "You can't judge classical singing, and that money is for the Voice Faculty." I said "You are aware that I am part of the Voice Faculty. I don't belong to Musical Theatre"?
R:	What did she say to that?
AG:	She did not respond. Just left ... then shortly after, maybe even a year or two after, I don't remember, I saw on Facebook, um, because I mean PGG upstairs, we get together occasionally, as a group, PGG, BG, QGG (Head of Voice). And, um, PGG had posted a picture at RGG's house, he's right next door to me here *(in the office next door)* who lives kinda where I do, of a big summer gathering. "Oh look, can you believe that we got all of the University G Voice Faculty together." So, I showed that to my partner, tried not to get weepy, and he said, "You can't let that bother you." I said, "I'm trying so hard not to let it bother me." Because I don't want to be like the little kid that's standing outside on the playground! I mean that's just ...
R:	Mm
AG:	I said, it just brings everything to the head, and that makes me cranky. So, I then had a talk to PGG. I said "PGG, I really need to talk to you because I have to just verbalise this." And she said, "You know, it wasn't intentional," I said "I realise it wasn't intentional, and I realise I don't come to any of your faculty meetings,

	you all have studio class, there is no time for my kids to have a studio class, I understand. But, no. No."
	At this point AG has tears in her eyes.
R:	Are you invited to faculty meetings?
AG:	No, I don't even know when they have them.[11]

The exclusion and marginalisation from the larger voice pedagogy field that this teacher has experienced, *despite* having classical voice performance experience and appropriate qualifications and being a long serving member of faculty, is a powerful demonstration of how classical voice pedagogy dominates the field. There is a lack of consideration or even acknowledgement of the existence of those who practice other genres. Classical voice teachers use their symbolic power without an understanding of its presence (doxa). Not only do classical teachers not understand the presence of their power, there is also a lack of understanding of the effects this power exerts on others in the field. This field dominance results in not just the rather academic argument of linguistic exclusion, but *actual* pain and distress for those who have the appropriate capitals to position themselves within the field but who find themselves excluded and marginalised due to their practice in musical theatre or CCM genres.

This teacher was not alone in experiencing marginalisation by classical pedagogues. Examples of symbolic power used by classical colleagues on musical theatre teachers include a participant being booked for a masterclass on voice functionality, which was then cancelled upon the discovery that they worked in the musical theatre and not the classical department—the teacher was told "we wanted someone more opera".[12] One participant described sadness at giving up dance classes because they needed to focus on classical voice, rather than musical theatre which was not a study option. Teachers whose voice qualities did not meet the aesthetic standards of classical voice performance were not introduced to other singing genres where they might find a "fit" but were told they were failures and would never succeed professionally.

The need for civility

The nature of the field means that teachers don't necessarily admit these painful experiences easily. It is not "seemly" within voice pedagogy to complain too much about classical voice teachers' behaviour towards CCM colleagues as it can damage career prospects. Differentiating CCM voice function and style from classical is seen as an alternative, more diplomatic approach by CCM and musical theatre teachers to making space within the field of voice pedagogy for them and their work. It was through the de-identifying nature of this project that teachers felt safe to express the pain they had experienced at the hands of classical pedagogues who, perhaps unknowingly,[13] hold and use significant symbolic power in the field. Teachers who have been in the field for any length of time understand the politics of not upsetting their classical colleagues by pointing out the power imbalance in the field. Those who teach CCM and musical theatre singing discuss in private the need to take care of the egos of those who are in authority (classical voice pedagogues), to "get along" within the field and not stir up trouble.

The demonstration of the symbolic power of classical pedagogy is further illustrated by the need for musical theatre voice teachers to use their classical voice qualifications and experience as a defence against attacks on their credibility within the voice pedagogy field. Upon being asked what skills a prospective musical theatre voice teacher required; BX responded:

BX: Well, I would certainly encourage, it's a new age, it's a different age than it used to be, but I would certainly probably still tell that person to learn all they could about similarities and differences between classical singing and musical theatre contemporary music because the hoses are still aimed at you. Ah, and so you have to prove that you know the territory.

...

BX: So the other thing I would say is, if you can, get, I don't know what your background is, but become as comfortable as you can with demonstrating classical sounds too so, it's a defence, but if people are dubious about "oh you teach that" you can say "oh I also do this". So that you show that you're also teaching vocal versatility.[14]

The term "hoses are aimed at you" refers to civil rights protests against racist treatment by those in authority, who then perpetuated this injustice through the use of more violence against peaceful protesters.[15] While I am in **no way** comparing the treatment of CCM and musical theatre voice teachers to these racist injustices, it is interesting that this was the metaphor this teacher came up with to explain the experience was one accustomed to which describes pain caused by extreme injustice. The level of distress experienced by this teacher may not warrant the use of this term. I acknowledge this may be offensive to people of colour who have experienced institutionalised, structural, systemic political, and institutionally sanctioned racism and the very real harm this has caused individuals and groups of people. That these racist practices and injustice continue to this day not just in the United States but in many countries around the world, including my own country, is in my opinion, insupportable.

The participant's use of this term indicates a *perception* and experience of being under unjust attack simply for working in a different musical genre to classical. There is an expectation that the decision to move into the musical theatre genre is somehow only acceptable within the larger field if a teacher can demonstrate that they have classical performance and teaching skills, and that the musical theatre voice teacher should still expect to be on the receiving end of continued and sustained questioning of their credentials which can only be validated through the ability to teach classical voice styles, *as well* as musical theatre.

Further symbolic power is demonstrated within academia by classical faculty through the lack of provision of specialist musical theatre voice teachers for musical theatre majors. As I have stated previously, it would be difficult to consider the opposite, that is, a music programme being satisfied that a musical theatre voice specialist with little to no experience performing or training in classical style singing could appropriately train undergraduate students in classical voice, yet this still happens in musical theatre programmes. Here, the positioning of the deep structure of classical voice training as being an appropriate foundation for musical theatre performers feeds into symbolic power at these universities. The musical theatre voice teachers at one university commented that they spent the first six months to a year with second year (sophomore) students undoing the first year of classical training to get the voices set up for musical theatre singing. There is a lack of understanding shown by the classical academy to their musical theatre colleagues in their belief that not only should they (classical voice specialists) teach musical theatre majors without appropriate performance experience or training in the genre, but also a lack of understanding for the appropriate education of these students, the education that students are paying for and expect to be appropriate to their chosen discipline.

Symbolic capital, and the symbolic power used by those with the highest amounts of symbolic capital in the field of voice pedagogy means that those who have this power are affirmed in their work through the position they take within the social space of the field of voice pedagogy. Further, the students fortunate enough to be chosen to work with these powerful pedagogues are being prepared (or as Bourdieu would call it, ordained) to replicate the field as it stands. The scarcity of universities offering CCM credentials means that there is little competition to the status quo, as the power base for this industry is founded on the educational capital provided by academic appointments which in turn are reinforced through professional body membership and executive positions, which then further reinforce what is considered scholarly and worthy of investigation.

While younger participant teachers did not experience the same level of offense at the symbolic power used by classical colleagues that older participants in the study experienced, these younger participants were buffeted somewhat by their high educational capital (doctoral degrees) and by being able to adeptly speak the language of both classical and musical theatre. Additionally, they were newer to academia and focused on setting up productive relationships with their classical colleagues. One participant mentioned that *because* she was classically trained and had "classical chops" she was well-respected by her classical colleagues. While these younger teachers had not experienced the pain of having symbolic power used in both social and professional situations (yet), they were at the same time careful to acknowledge that they had access to positive relationships through their existing cultural and symbolic (performance) capital.

Practice: The intersection of habitus and capital within the field of musical theatre voice teaching

The following case study provides one way of understanding the research conclusions by examining how an individual's practice can be constituted through habitus and capital interacting within the field of voice pedagogy. In terms of habitus, the teacher identified as a white female who was encouraged into the arts within her early home life. As a child she performed in a musical theatre, and commented "I was primarily a dancer, I was a much stronger dancer than singer ... I loved it ... I viewed it as a hobby".[16] She was enrolled in a double degree, and was planning on moving into a medical career when:

> The [music] faculty basically cornered me and said, "are you considering, seriously considering a career in music?" and I said "no, that's ridiculous, I'm not going to do that." And they said "well, we think you should reconsider. Um, and we think you have what it takes, and we think that you should seriously consider this."[17]

As a direct result of this encouragement by classical music faculty, she completed an undergraduate music performance programme, and then auditioned for and was accepted to "a top five classical conservatory"[18] for a master's degree in classical voice performance. This was followed by a DMA in classical vocal performance in yet another classical programme. The teacher possessed considerable cultural capital in the form of educational capital through postgraduate training in prestigious institutions. Her master's and doctoral degrees were displayed on the walls of her teaching studio. The acquisition of high-level educational (cultural) capital was encouraged and supported through habitus through the early family encouragement which provided access (financial, time) to performance and training opportunities in dance and musical theatre, as well as exposure to choir singing.

Following graduation from the doctoral programme, she progressed into voice teaching and discovered that she needed to know how to teach musical theatre to meet the student needs in her private studio. While she could capably teach and perform legit-style musical theatre, she needed to retrain. Accordingly, she took additional training from a private teacher and explored various short pedagogical training courses in CCM and musical theatre voice performance. Interestingly, contradicting many other lessons I observed, this teacher in practice did not appear to expect musical theatre students to engage in classical music at all. She focused equally on music theatre and CCM genres within lessons and structured the voice syllabus in the musical theatre programme so that classical performance was not a requirement. She used the toolbox of resources she had learnt from attending CCM-specific professional development training outside of her university-based degrees to work with students on CCM style and function. The classical degrees from highly respected institutions may have assisted her to gain entry to an academic post, but additional training was required to provide the skills necessary to practice in an appropriate manner within the musical theatre field.

In terms of the field of voice pedagogy, this teacher came to her position without a Broadway or national touring history in musical theatre, however she did have performance experience in regional legit musical theatre productions. She did have prestigious classical performance experience which could be turned into cultural capital in the larger field of voice pedagogy. She commented that "in my generation I feel like my colleagues who teach only classical voice are rooting for me. I feel like it's a supportive integrated inclusive community". However, she also noted:

> in the larger voice community, I know that a lot of CCM teachers and, ah, music theatre teachers are not treated equally. I know that there is a lot of prejudice, and that there is, um, a lot of CCM bashing that goes on in the classical community. There is a tremendously strong bias, still, that comes out of ignorance and I recognise that it's not necessarily people trying to be mean or exclusive ... it's very easy in academia, it's not easy in independent voice teaching, but in academia to still perceive the world as mostly classical, with just a hint of musical theatre, and in the actual field of how much work is available for your students when they graduate from a program, you know, it's the other way. ... academia has been privileged by support of an institution and so they've been able to preserve a world view that has expired. So, so I think that that atmosphere contributes to sort of a wilful ignorance, you know, a sort of wilful denial of what the field actually looks like. And that's the reason I didn't want a classical job.[19]

132 *The field of voice pedagogy*

AM felt supported as a musical theatre and CCM teacher because she had transitioned from a classical culture to the other styles, commenting "because I came out of classical conservatory, and I have **three** degrees, I have the street cred with the classical people". AM's considerable classical training was certainly used to provide her with legitimacy within the larger voice community, as opposed to those teachers without this background who get "bashed" by the classical community. The hierarchy of the voice pedagogy community is clearly expressed and recognised by this teacher, and her educational and cultural capitals provide her with a competency which allows her to move freely within it, giving her "street cred" with classical colleagues who are at the top of the hierarchical field of voice pedagogy.

Notes

1 Bourdieu & Wacquant, 1992, p. 97.
2 Thomson, 2008.
3 Bourdieu, 1979/2010, p. 473.
4 University of South Carolina: Instructor of Voice-Soprano, April 2020.
5 National Centre for Education Statistics, 2019.
6 Shulman, 2005.
7 Deer, 2008.
8 Ibid., p. 121.
9 Ibid., p. 119.
10 American Academy of Teachers of Singing, 2008.
11 Interview transcription, University G.
12 Interview transcription, University X.
13 Whether this power is used knowingly or not would be an interesting study. Who a particular person in the field has time to talk to and who they choose to remember may be power strategy designed to improve a teacher's position within the field.
14 Interview transcription, University X.
15 As an Australian I was not familiar with this term. Photographic evidence of this practice may be viewed here: www.loc.gov/item/201 4645234/
16 Interview transcription, University M, participant AM.
17 Interview transcription, University M, participant AM.
18 Ibid.
19 Interview transcription, University M, teacher AM.

References

American Academy of Teachers of Singing. (2008). *In support of Contemporary Commercial Music (nonclassical) voice pedagogy.* www.americanacademyofteachersofsinging.org/assets/articles/CCMVoicePedagogy.pdf

Bourdieu, P. (2010). *Distinction: A social critique of the judgement of taste* (R. Nice, Trans). Routledge. (Original work published 1979).

Bourdieu P., & Wacquant, L. (1992). *An invitation to reflexive sociology.* Polity.

Deer, C., (2008). Doxa. In M. Grenfell (Ed.), *Pierre Bourdieu: Key concepts* (pp. 119–130). Acumen.

National Centre for Education Statistics. (2019). *Race/ethnicity of college faculty.* https://nces.ed.gov/fastfacts/display.asp?id=61

Shulman, L. (2005). Signature pedagogies in the professions. *Daedalus, 134*(3), 52–59.

Thomson, P., (2008). Field. In M. Grenfell (Ed.), *Pierre Bourdieu: Key concepts* (pp. 67–81). Acumen.

8 Turning the corner?

The research underpinning the discussions in this book was conducted prior to the Covid pandemic. The pandemic played out unevenly across the world, and the field of voice pedagogy was not excluded from huge disruption. Movement towards online teaching occurred quickly, and it was a fascinating time to observe the field as I wrote up this research. The following is based on my observations of the field as of the time of writing, through the conceptual lens of my research.

The Covid impact

The Covid pandemic, at first glance, may have appeared to have levelled the playing field somewhat, as university academics and private voice teachers across all styles scurried to deliver online teaching. Online teaching, once an optional extra for many institutions, became imperative to university teaching models. This delivery mode was used to maintain enrolments, an important consideration for the financial security of universities in the United States particularly as they approach a projected enrolment decline due to approaching demographic changes.[1] Online delivery created continuity for delivery of educational outcomes and sustained interpersonal connections during the pandemic.

The field of voice pedagogy remains strongly structured following the Covid pandemic. A journal article regarding the post-pandemic voice pedagogue serves as an example of how the systems and structures established prior to Covid remain firmly in place.[2] The author began the article by affirming his academic

DOI: 10.4324/9781003332572-8

credentials, employment, and lineage; bona fides (educational, cultural, symbolic, and scientific capital) which serve to affirm his status in the field as a player of some standing. Affirmation of capitals provide validation for this opinion piece, and by extension, those who he (and this organisation) advises.

While applauding the accessibility of knowledge due to the explosion of online resources, the article simultaneously marginalises those who teach singing or promote online learning and singing, outside of the playing space (social space, field, cultural game) of the membership of the organisation represented by a specific journal readership. The author advises the reader "in an oversaturated environment, we must choose discerningly". Who is the "we"? Those playing and in power within the social space of voice pedagogy. This includes those in positions of authority to write and be published, to hold executive office, and to speak at conferences run by the organisation. Why is the online environment "oversaturated"? Because it is not curated by those who hold the power in the field. Those who are appropriately credentialled generally determine what is published and thereby validated. The author advises those in the field playing the cultural game (by reading the journal article) that a particular organisation (membership in the playing field) is "helpful, assisting teachers in sorting through and affirming what is most relevant and useful".[3] This language is linguistic evidence of the traditional power structures asserted in the online environment. Those in power in this organisation (social structure, playing field) are the ones who can direct their membership (participants in the game) towards the voices which "should" be heard, and by implication, who is to be avoided and excluded.

Regarding the field of voice pedagogy, the author encourages the reader that "we must ... earnestly engage in outreach efforts with our colleagues in the larger profession".[4] Where is the "larger profession"? This is an implicit statement that the voice pedagogy field is a specific game with specific players. The term "larger profession" implies there may be more voice teachers off the playing field, outside of the group of academic voice pedagogues represented by the author. It may be that those outside the playing field don't even know it exists, or don't particularly care that there is a field of voice teachers writing about voice pedagogy.[5] Or it may be that teachers outside the field, especially contemporary and/or musical theatre teachers, choose not to engage because despite calls for equality of music inclusiveness,[6] they are frustrated with constantly seeing those who have a classical background promoted in the field, as the author asserts by overtly providing his classical credentials and lineage without acknowledging the privilege of these capitals.

In this article, linguistic affirmation serves to maintain the status quo where classical voice pedagogy dominates. While admirable in intention, the exhortation that "recitals" include music by underrepresented artists is further example of this dominance. Contemporary singers and musical theatre performers do not generally give recitals. They perform at concerts (CCM and musical theatre) and showcases (musical theatre students in academia). The author also reports his personal response to the experience of teaching through the pandemic. The pandemic allowed him to "move at a slower pace".[7] This is the privilege of being a classically trained, tenured professor with an income which continued despite the pandemic, as opposed to private teachers whose business suffered due to student loss, or the inability to work online from home. This article is a reassertion that the social space of voice pedagogy literature is largely dominated by those classically trained and employed by the university sector, with access to this work in HME via their classical credentials.

Why does this matter? Because this journal is the voice of the largest body of singing teacher educators in the United States and this author was recently promoted to editor of voice pedagogy. Since the author began the article by stating his considerable classical education credentials, scholarship, and lineage, it is an example of the way in which these qualifications and lineage are used to reproduce, validate, and reaffirm the social structures of the voice pedagogy field. Those in positions of power within the field position themselves and deploy their capitals to assert the authority of their opinions and thereby reproduce the field. This is a clear dominance of the field by classically trained academics, considering, again, that classical voice performance makes up such a small percentage of the music consumed in the United States.[8]

Gender equity, Covid, and voice pedagogy

Safety of singers and teachers was understandably of paramount focus as the pandemic emerged. The urgency to understand the

Turning the corner? 137

impacts of this airborne disease[9] justifiably focused research on the impacts of the illnesses caused by Covid on singers.[10] This type of research has been privileged over social and gender issues when it comes to investigating the impact of Covid in the field of voice pedagogy. It is well documented that the pandemic had considerably more severe impact on female careers than men.[11] While the gendered impact of Covid worldwide has been a subject of considerable interest and research, at the time of writing, this subject is largely missing from scholarship in the voice pedagogy field.

Classical content in musical theatre degrees

The initial aim of this study was to explore how singing teachers in select universities in the United States apply CCM singing pedagogy in the instruction of musical theatre students. I began this research because I wanted to know the answers to these questions both for the field of voice pedagogy and for my own practice. From my readings I could see that musical theatre had a place of greater prominence in the literature than other contemporary singing styles. I suspected musical theatre was perceived to be more academically legitimate by stakeholders in the field of voice pedagogy in the United States. From a political standpoint, I wondered if by illuminating the ways in which CCM styles were being taught in musical theatre practice in academia, that I might contribute to the legitimisation of teaching CCM voice pedagogy within academia.

From afar, I had trouble reconciling the comparatively small amount of research-based literature in CCM practices when compared with classical voice practices. For the past 22 years I have operated a business and taught in secondary and tertiary institutions where I have taught exclusively CCM and musical theatre singing. During this time only one student has requested a classical-style training. I hoped that perhaps this research might contribute to the growing body of literature into CCM, specifically focusing in on voice training within academia. I learnt enormous amounts about different approaches and applications of pedagogical skill to teaching voice through observing my participants, and their impact on my teaching resonates through my practice.

After observing the amount of classical teaching in observed musical theatre teaching practices, I questioned why this classical content was so present in music theatre degrees. Shouldn't music theatre students receive the same level of expert, focused training on the repertoire they will be *required* to perform as professionals in musical theatre as classical students receive in their degrees? I do not mean to imply that students I observed were *not* receiving focused training on musical theatre singing repertoire and style, in fact, the opposite. The teaching of specific music theatre singing function and repertoire was practiced across all research sites. However, I did observe considerable time in lessons spent at some institutions on classical repertoire and function. This appeared to be at the expense of time spent working on CCM repertoire and technical work. Cross training *function* associated with classical singing has skill acquisition value particularly in consideration of elite musical theatre belting. This functional training can develop skilled vibrato and ring, elements of singing traditionally associated with classical training rather than CCM training.[12] However, wouldn't time spent on voice qualities and functions present in the other CCM styles currently dominating music theatre be at least as useful, if not more useful than time spent on classical voice repertoire and foreign language study? Perhaps teachers are simply teaching what they know, what they were taught, without consideration of what students may require in the industry now? Or does the classical world require additional classically trained singers to maintain the art form due a lack of classically trained performers in their industry? I suspect this is not the case.

The impact of not teaching CCM styles to musical theatre students

Knowledge and competence of CCM styles are important for musical theatre singers but there is a continued long-standing assumption that these styles are simple to produce and do not require specialised instruction. I was recently involved in a situation where I was asked by a music director to help "rough up" a voice to sound more authentically CCM in a music theatre studio class. This request assumes that CCM technique involves a quick and easy fix, rather than skills acquired through practice and training (just like classical voice technique). If a student has not been taught functionally safe ways of vocalising stylistically in voice lessons (with the understanding of the impact of amplification on the ability to make this sound with ease and vocal safety in performance) and is given directions like this in an audition or rehearsal room, what are they to do? It is in just this kind of situation that vocal damage may occur.

I believe that as educators we should be training students adequately for the profession they wish to enter, **whatever** that is. While all the sites I visited taught musical theatre style and function, the additional focus on classical repertoire, especially when teachers did not include CCM function and repertoire training, might lead to inadequate career preparation for students. The following is a reflection following a lesson with a recent graduate from a musical theatre programme in the United States:

> Today I worked with M, a student who has just graduated from a musical theatre degree. We have online lessons as she is living in New York and attending many auditions and performance opportunities each week. We have gone through her audition book and realised that she has many gaps, lots of songs which are inappropriate for her age and voice, and not enough golden age repertoire despite her considerable classical training within her musical theatre degree. She told me today she was at an audition where she sang a Disney song, and then the audition panel saw she had a Whitney Houston song in her book. They asked her to sing it, and she did, but knew something wasn't right—the panel reaction wasn't what she had hoped for. She asked me for help with it. She sang the song, and it was all in her head register. We talked about what people might expect to hear from a Whitney Houston song and experimented with finding her chest register in the lower notes. Once she did this, the belt appeared naturally into the top of her voice. She commented "that felt right!" and it sounded right too.[13]

This excerpt demonstrates the loss of opportunity for this one student in this audition. She held a Bachelor of Musical Theatre degree. She had saved to move to New York and audition for professional work. However, she did not have the training to sing CCM styles with appropriate function or authentic style. She also had gaps in her audition book and didn't know how the repertoire she did have needed to be prepared for professional auditions. Her repertoire choices for auditions highlighted her lack of skill in a particular area—her understanding of the requirements of contemporary singing. This example illustrates the cost of inappropriate training in just one undergraduate student. She was paying for additional lessons and had sought me out as a CCM specialist *after* graduation.

In this case, the student's teacher at university *did* have a classical voice performance background and *did not* prepare the student adequately for auditions. From my experience in the United States, I know that many music theatre voice teachers, including the participants in this study, were initially trained in classical voice performance and *are* extremely skilled at teaching musical theatre style, function, and repertoire preparation. They have sought out additional training opportunities and become experts in their field. They have built practices into their teaching which are more inclusive of CCM and musical theatre requirements than they themselves received. However, the above example demonstrates that there are voice teachers working in the musical theatre field in academia who have *not* been exposed to, or sought out, additional pedagogical training. The dissonance between the background and training of musical theatre voice teachers and the requirements of their practice, if not actively addressed, continues the cycle, reproducing the same voice problems in newly graduated students. This impacts on the future teaching profession, because students in the performing arts often become teachers themselves.[14]

Impacts of classical music dominance in academia

While I am, as are, I suspect, all voice teachers, highly interested in the nitty-gritty of *how* we teach, I soon realised that the more important, in fact urgent, topic to be examined here was not the provision of more "how-tos" in terms of musical theatre and CCM teaching. Although I collected a huge quantity of data containing considerable information on various technical approaches, the broader, philosophical discussion about the way voice training currently operates within academia emerged as an important issue. I considered my final two research questions—how the educational background of teachers assists them in their work, and how CCM-specific pedagogical training assisted teachers in their teaching—and realised I had heard a similar story from each of the participants I interviewed. Despite previous literature into the lack of the type of long-term focused training in CCM pedagogy available within the United States,[15] I did not think that I would encounter an almost complete dominance of graduate and undergraduate classical voice performance backgrounds in *musical theatre* voice teachers.

It was common for participants to have completed nine to ten years of academic level classical training for those teachers with a doctorate, or six years for those with a master's degree, only to require retraining to teach musical theatre styles. In terms of other CCM styles, some teachers described attending short courses to gain understanding of these singing styles. However, I believe that a two- to nine-day short course in teaching CCM does not equip teachers adequately into the nuances of CCM singing and teaching. Indeed, this training seems tokenistic when compared with an extremely long immersive classical education. It is certainly not the "in-depth study" of stylistically appropriate pedagogical training for singing teachers called for by the American Academy of Teachers of Singing.[16] These courses are, however, a very useful *introduction* to contemporary singing function, stylistic nuances, and aesthetics.

The third and fourth research questions projected the research from the specifics of individual participant experiences in their background and training, to the examination of a discernible pattern within the total group of participants. The *impact* of classical voice pedagogy dominance in academia on current teaching practice is here considered. When teachers began to disclose to me the personal costs of their experiences both in training and at the hands of their classical colleagues, whether in interviews or informal conversations, I was moved. Participants commented that they disclosed these matters *only* because they knew they and their schools would be de-identified. The novel use of multi-sited focused ethnography was essential to this research study.[17] This methodology enabled participants to feel safe enough to tell their stories—their experiences were heard and validated, rather than minimised or blamed on their inability to "make it" in the classical world. The reluctance of teachers to acknowledge the difficulties they had experienced both in training and after graduation without anonymisation is also indicative of the very real power dynamics at play within the field and within the academy.

To openly discuss problems experienced due to inappropriate training was perceived by participants as a "no go" zone. To discuss pedagogical shortcomings of training, or differences in pedagogical approach was tacitly understood to be potentially antagonising their classical colleagues. Classical music pedagogues must be "managed" by CCM pedagogues in academia to gradually acknowledge there is a legitimate place for CCM and musical theatre styles, and that this is not *instead* of classical (indicating that perhaps there is a fear from classical colleagues that CCM will "take over"), but *alongside* classical. Due to the institutional power that classically focused music performance education possesses in academia, musical theatre teachers implicitly understood that they must play by the "rules of the game". Classical colleagues hold considerable power not just in the field, through and within academia, but also by individuals through the careful relationships which are required for musical theatre teachers to maintain and hold their positions.

When music departments are called to diversify their offerings to students, questions arise about quality. How does a teacher trained and experienced in one genre measure the quality of singing for examination purposes required by academia when assessing singing performed in different styles and genres? The privilege of classical voice pedagogy within the field is shifting. Participants described joining departments with a majority of classically trained voice faculty and learning that deference was required when discussing the specific differences of their student's singing genres. Careful choice of language and paying tribute to the skills and tradition of excellence in classical singing were required. Management of classical voice teacher egos occurs when contemporary and musical theatre-focused teachers discuss pedagogy with classical colleagues at conferences, in faculty meetings, and in online forums.

Demonstrating the significant power structures within departments, participants described colleagues who had tenure and considerable power dismissing the specific requirements of musical theatre singing. While these teachers exist within the system (and a tenured faculty member will generally be in their position until retirement) shifts within academic voice pedagogy culture may be glacially slow. Understandably, nobody wants to feel like their skills, which have given them a performance and teaching career, are no longer relevant. However, the considerable weight of history and the upholding of Western classical music as the standard bearer for excellence remains, along with the exclusionary practices of structural racism[18] and gender biases. Newer teachers without tenure described walking a tightrope between advocating for student needs and keeping their colleagues onside. They experienced this difficult work environment while also being dismissed, overlooked, and openly disrespected by their classical colleagues. They described painful experiences of being perceived as having less skill (despite their own considerable classical training), or only being acceptable to their classical colleagues *because* of their classical skills and background—despite not teaching these styles. However, for these teachers to remain in their positions, they were required to position themselves within the field as "less than" their classical colleagues in their workplaces, at conferences and in online forums.

While writing about the "how-to" of teaching CCM is very welcome within the voice pedagogy community (and this is what I thought would be the subject of my research), from an outsider's perspective there appears to be a general reluctance in voice performance education in the United States to take a step back and examine the broader philosophical picture of the field of singing voice education. When participants engaged me in conversation about their experiences in the larger field of voice pedagogy, particularly the ways in which they had been "put in their place" by classical colleagues, I got the impression that this topic is "the elephant in the room" for many musical theatre voice teachers, particularly those sensitive to maintaining a positive working environment and who have experienced some kind of marginalisation by their classical colleagues.

Some participant teachers' educational experiences were distressing and hurtful. Participants described paying for an education only to be told they could not learn the genre they expected to be taught or being advised that was something inherently "wrong" with their voice's natural sound quality, without any suggestion of an alternative professional pathway or other kind of professional advice given. As an outsider, this kind of educational experience appeared to be highly unethical. Problematic experiences were often framed as being a deficiency in the student, not the teacher, and certainly not the fault of a system which upholds a classical aesthetic. As one participant commented:

> I did not ever understand what she was talking about. And so, I was **so** confused in every lesson, I just knew I wasn't doing

what she wanted but I didn't for the life of me understand what she wanted. And I wanted so much to please her, and I couldn't do it, and so I was **very** discouraged, and I just was extremely frustrated.[19]

Interestingly, one hallmark of this participant's teaching practice was a clarity of instruction and a positive affirmation of the student's responses to instruction. Smith and Powell[20] comment that "people's experiences of education are frequently self-defining and life-changing—affirming, uplifting, crushing, celebratory and (dis)empowering by turns". Participants' experiences within the academic classical music environment cut deeply, impacting on both their approach to their teaching practices (both positively and negatively) and their self-perceptions of their positions with the voice pedagogy field.

Changing the field—looking forward with hope

While there was a commonality of negative experiences, my analysis revealed that change may be occurring quickly. One participant, who worked in a small regional university with only three voice teachers on staff to teach musical theatre, described waiting for a colleague to retire:

> Um, my previous colleague ... is very much a classical snob, and she says it, and she's very proud of that. Um, she hates this, and she hates that, um, and she loved to criticise the stuff that I did.[21]

However, as teachers retire, a new generation of teachers move into academia hopefully with more inclusive attitudes. When I asked this participant about his experiences with the voice pedagogy community at large he responded:

> I feel like the "classical only" teachers are only jealous of, you know, are like "what am I missing?" And I don't got to a lot of NATS events, but I remember the last one I went to was two summers ago in Chicago, and teachers were, I remember asking how many, I can't remember what session we were in, "How many of you, you know, teach, have at least one, you know,

teach some musical theatre?" and every hand raises. "Now how many of you don't teach any classical students?" and I mean, a third to a half, I mean, a lot of teachers.[22]

Interestingly, another teacher with a strong background in classical training felt strongly that teaching and singing contemporary singing requires *more* skill than teaching classical. I asked this participant what they felt the most important considerations were when teaching CCM voice and they replied:

> Number one: It's one voice. Um, it's one larynx, its one mechanism. In CCM they *have* to be flexible enough and have access to **all** the different colours that that mechanism offers. Even more than, **definitely** more than classical. Even more than musical theatre. It has to, it has to be totally versatile, in my opinion. Um, which requires in their training that they have the ability to go from one full sound to another full sound and every single shade in between. Um, so I almost consider it, you know a lot of people think opera is the highest form, I'm like, if you do CCM, OK. musical theatre the next step and then opera. I consider it, like opera training is here *(holds hands out a bit)*, musical theatre training we have to make it here *(hands open wider apart)*, CCM we have to make it here *(arms are fully extended)*. I consider it the opposite. That CCM should really be able to do everything that encompasses all the others.[23]

As the market has changed and the singing teachers have had to adjust with it, they are discovering the complexities and different requirements of both CCM and musical theatre singing.

In 2005, renowned, trailblazing CCM pedagogue Robert Edwin hopefully commented on the need for "college and university voice pedagogy courses to include Contemporary Commercial Music voice technique and repertoire in the syllabus. Initially many would have to go outside their departments to find experienced and qualified instructors in that area".[24] Where to find this inclusion, and where those suitably qualified[25] and experienced teachers come from, appear to still be relevant questions to ask many years later. Changes to academia can be extraordinarily slow-moving. The tenure process in the United States may have something to do with this. If the music department has tenured professors of classical voice, it is difficult to adjust to changes in demand as classical enrolments fall. These professors are still being paid to teach voice, and they are experts in classical voice, so that is what their programme offers. If a programme needs to change to attract students, the foundations for their careers may be under threat. Further, not all teachers want to learn a new pedagogy, especially when they have years of experience and validation as an expert in their specific, narrow field.

Like Edwin,[26] I am hopeful that a shift towards inclusivity of other styles, taught by those who are expert in these styles, who "live in" and perform these styles, *and* have pedagogical qualifications (rather than voice teachers with a classical voice default) is underway. I acknowledge that many institutions in the United States are moving towards inclusivity through recruitment of teachers with some CCM teaching experience. However, the classical default remains while there are so few graduate programmes committed to teaching CCM voice pedagogy and performance as its own degree. If one considers the accessibility of high-quality contemporary music education in higher education with the availability of classical music education, it appears clear that the system will continue to produce mostly classical voice performers, some of whom will continue into academic teaching careers.

It might be contended that there are graduate programmes which include music theatre and CCM styles as a *part* of a programme, for example, one semester course within a larger degree. However, Reinhert[27] discusses the difficulty of fitting in everything required of a professional CCM performer within the traditional academic structure of an undergraduate degree. This assertion regarding undergraduate CCM requirements alone indicates that expert CCM voice pedagogy for teachers is not a side note, not something that can be taught in a nine-day summer programme (useful those these may be), and not something a performer can become expert in across a one semester course within a programme.

Pedagogical training for future voice teachers and performers wishing to focus on CCM styles needs to be taken as seriously and positioned in the same way as a classical music degree. Why does this matter? First, because these undergraduate and graduate performance degree majors deserve to be taught by experts in their field. Second, if history repeats itself, and students go on to become teachers, we *need* teachers who are deeply engaged with and well-trained in style specificity. A classical voice performance degree, whether undergraduate, master's or doctoral, affords the student excellent cultural capital within the field of voice pedagogy and gives access to potential academic employment. However, *if* it doesn't prepare them with the appropriate skills and knowledge for future employment either as a performer or teacher in their *preferred* field, this kind of education is a disservice to the student.

The implications of including CCM as a discipline in its own right within music performance departments suggests, somewhat controversially, that classical is not at the top of the hierarchy within voice pedagogy but simply another discipline itself, and not innately superior to CCM or musical theatre singing styles. This does not need to be an oppositional paradigm,[28] and I am not interested in rehashing the contemporary versus classical culture wars. However, including CCM as a field in music performance education at the undergraduate level in more music departments in the United States is a way to increase music performance education participation in light of falling enrolments in classical music programmes.[29] A contemporary music performance department sitting alongside a classical department could provide the additional expert training future voice pedagogy students require, as well as providing the appropriate education for those performers interested in CCM or music theatre singing.

At the beginning of this research process, I pondered how it was classical voice performance dominates academic music study in the United States, despite this style of music being based on a Western European tradition. Music which originated in the United States—rock, country, pop, jazz, musical theatre, and R&B—are not necessarily included as a matter of course in the training of singers. Yet these genres are very popular not only with the general public of the United States but have been exported around the world. Since I started this research, I have read more about the inherent gender discrimination systems and racism upholding the Western classical music canon as a standard of excellence within higher music education in the United States.[30]

However, change is occurring, although in slow and sometimes unexpected places. I have experienced first-hand how classical music itself is changing in academia to address Eurocentrism and racism inherent in academic music study. I was fortunate to attend a recent, powerfully joyful performance of groundbreaking composer and flautist Valerie Coleman's music through The [REPRESENT]atoire Project.[31] What was particularly moving was the discussion with Coleman and the students who worked on the project. One young female musician involved in the project commented that she had received *ten years* of music instruction before being given a piece of music to learn which was composed by a woman.[32] The student who instigated the residency of Coleman, Diamond Gaston, commented that when needing assistance with embouchure as an aspiring flautist she searched online for someone who looked like her. This search took hours.[33] Women, people of colour, people with neuro-divergence, and people from diverse backgrounds must be represented within the music taught in higher education. The culture of music in higher education is largely classical, Eurocentric (white), and dominated by male composers. While changes *are* happening in the higher music education, cultural change is slow. Events like *The [Represent]atoire Project* provide hope for a more inclusive musical education for those who study classical music.

This experience mirrors what my generous participants demonstrated—change is possible. Classically trained teachers, if they are interested, are well able to learn how to teach both musical theatre and CCM genres with additional professional development. There will always be those classical voice teachers who do not want to teach musical theatre or CCM singing. These teachers, whose aesthetic disposition regard CCM and musical theatre styles as something they do not wish to engage with in their practice, are necessary. We need such experts to ensure classical music education continues to engage those performers who prefer classical genres.

If it is true that "the singing teacher is the most important person ... for any developing singer",[34] then the appropriate education of aspiring voice teachers is imperative. Providing increased undergraduate and graduate courses focused on CCM and musical theatre voice pedagogy and performance will create a change in the culture of voice pedagogy in the United States. Many of these potential new teachers will enter graduate courses from CCM performance backgrounds without the current requisite classical performance skills. Universities may need to consider adjusting audition requirements to welcome these students into graduate

Turning the corner? 149

voice pedagogy programmes. Programme directors may need to consider what pedagogical subjects may be taught across singing all genres (physiology, anatomy, acoustics, technology, history, educational theories) and what subjects require individualised tuition to create skilled practitioners (one-to-one voice lessons and workshops with experienced and qualified CCM and/or musical theatre singing teachers). Respect for CCM and musical theatre voice teachers will come with equal opportunity to study and conduct research at the highest levels in academia. The creation of master's and doctoral programmes with flexibility for part time and online study would create pathways for many teachers who already have thriving studios to access the benefits that academic credentials provide. Online coursework may be supplemented by in-house summer intensives for these students.

While this study is specific to a particular group of musical theatre voice teachers in the United States, the findings may be relevant to voice pedagogy internationally. Tertiary musical theatre programmes are present in many countries worldwide—established programmes exist in the United Kingdom, Australia, Europe, the Middle East, and Asia. Musical theatre productions are often exported internationally, and expectations of vocal sounds may be well-established through cast recordings prior to an international casting. Singing voice educators in both academia and the private studio in other countries are often expected to assist musical theatre performers to produce CCM vocal sounds and may find themselves with similar training, pedagogical and performance backgrounds to participants in this study.

The research underpinning the thoughts and conceptual framework of this book illuminated the state of play in the specific field of musical theatre voice pedagogy in a specific group of educators, in a specific time and place. My copy of Bourdieu's *Distinction* has travelled with me on this journey, and many times reassured me that:

> It is possible to enter into the singularity of an object without renouncing the ambition of drawing out universal propositions. It is … (by treating) its object as a "particular case of the possible", that one can hope to avoid unjustifiably universalizing the particular case.[35]

This was a "particular" study, and all findings must be read in the context of the ethnography which produced the data for analysis. The initial study produced thick rich data which when analysed through the conceptual framework of Bourdieu's concepts of habitus, capitals, and practice, allowed for the consideration of broader, deeper issues within the field which I have extended to include post-pandemic considerations. I am hopeful for a more egalitarian field, where the distinctions between styles are celebrated and appreciated in all their individual complexity. Lastly, and most fervently, I am hopeful that the academic validation process is opened up to the *whole* discipline of voice pedagogy.

Notes

1 Carey, 2021.
2 Hoch, 2022.
3 Ibid., p. 485.
4 Ibid., p. 486.
5 In the interests of full disclosure, I ran a large, successful business for 20 years as a private voice teacher working largely outside of academia. I began my research as a private teacher, working from home with children and family responsibilities. I have since taken up a tenure track position in the United States teaching CCM and musical theatre singing. I am aware of the ways of being both outside of academia and within academic hierarchical spaces.
6 Benson et al., 2021.
7 Hoch, 2022, p. 487.
8 Nielson, 2019.
9 Miller et al., 2021.
10 Meyer et al., 2021.
11 Bateman & Ross, 2020; Braund, 2020; Crabb, 2020; Pan American Health Organisation, 2021; United Nations Entity for Gender Equality and the Empowerment of Women (UN Women) United Nations Secretariat, 2020.
12 DeLeo LeBorgne et al., 2009.
13 Reflexive diary, Thursday, 12th September 2019.
14 Bennett & Bridgestock, 2015; Bennett et al., 2015.
15 DeSilva, 2016.
16 American Academy of Teachers of Singing, 2008.
17 Cox & Forbes, 2022.
18 Benson et al., 2021; Kajikawa, 2019; Wicks, 1998.
19 Interview transcription, University M.

Turning the corner? 151

20 Smith & Powell, 2017, para. 5.
21 Interview transcription, University Q.
22 Interview transcription, University Q.
23 Interview transcription, University T.
24 Edwin, 2005, p. 292.
25 Remembering that most universities require a masters or doctorate in a specialist field for a candidate to be considered qualified for employment.
26 Edwin, 2005.
27 Reinhert, 2020.
28 Smith et al., 2018.
29 Edwards, 2018.
30 Almqvist & Werner, 2022; Baldwin, November 2, 2020; Benson et al., 2021; Feder & McGill, 2021; Griffiths, 2019; Kajikawa, 2019; Overland, 2016; Sergeant & Himonides, 2022; Wicks, 1998.
31 The [REPRESENT]atoire Project, 10–11 November 2022, Coastal Carolina University.
32 Comments by Hailey Cornell at The [REPRESENT]atoire Project concert, 11 November 2022, Edwards College of Humanities and Fine Arts, Recital Hall, Coastal Carolina University.
33 Gaston, Diamond, quoted by Joshua Carroll. 17 November 2022. "[Represent]atoire project continues." *The Chanticleer.*
34 King & Nix, 2019, p. 695.
35 Bourdieu, 1979/2010, p. xiii.

References

Almqvist, C., & Werner, A. (February, 2022). Gender in Higher Music Education. PRIhME Assembly 2 [Expert Paper]. Association Européene des Conservatoires, Académies de Musique et Musikhochschulen (AEC). https://aec-music.eu/media/2022/03/2nd-Assembly-Brief.pdf

American Academy of Teachers of Singing. (2008). *In support of Contemporary Commercial Music (nonclassical) voice pedagogy.* www.americanacademyofteachersofsinging.org/assets/articles/CCMVoicePedagogy.pdf

Baldwin, J. (November 2, 2020). Teaching CCM Styles, Finding Your Voice, and Appropriating Styles…and Yourself // Dr. Trineice Robinson-Martin. *Singing in Popular Musics.* https://singinginpopularmusics.com/2020/11/02/teaching-ccm-styles-finding-your-voice-and-appropriating-styles-and-yourself-dr-trineice-robinson-martin/

Bateman, N., & Ross, M. (2020). *Why has Covid-19 been especially harmful for working women?* www.brookings.edu/essay/why-has-covid-19-been-especially-harmful-for-working-women/

Bennett, D., & Bridgestock, R. (2015). The urgent need for career preview: Student expectations and graduate realities in music and dance. *International Journal of Music Education, 33*(3), 263–267.

Bennett, D., Richardson, S., Mahat, M., Coates, H., MacKinnon, P., & Schmidt, L. (2015, July 6–9). *Navigating uncertainty and complexity: Higher education and the dilemma of employability.* Paper presented at the 38th HERDSA Annual International Conference, Melbourne.

Benson, E. A., Robinson-Martin, T., & Naismith, M. (2021). Practicing equity, diversity, inclusion, and belonging in the singing voice studio. *Voice and Speech Review.* doi: 10.1080/23268263.2021.1964723

Bourdieu, P. (2010). *Distinction: A social critique of the judgement of taste* (R. Nice, Trans). Routledge. (Original work published 1979).

Braund, C. *More work, less care & still it's gendered. Women on Boards Australia,* www.womenonboards.net/en-au/news/more-work,-less-care-it-s-still-gendered.

Carey, K. (November 21, 2021). *The incredible shrinking future of college. Vox.com.* www.vox.com/the-highlight/23428166/college-enrollment-population-education-crash?SOPHOS-2022_11_25&sponsored=0&position=8&scheduled_corpus_item_id=51dc0a10-b5af-4e91-af92-780be67a5b76

Cox D., & Forbes, M. (2022). Introducing multi-sited focused ethnography for researching one-to-one (singing voice) pedagogy in higher education. *Music Education Research*, doi: 10.1080/14613808.2022.2138842

Crabb, A. (23 May, 2020). *Coronavirus has left Australian women anxious, overworked, insecure—and worse off than men again.* www.abc.net.au/news/2020-05-24/coronavirus-has-set-back-progress-for-women-workplace-equality/12268742

DeLeo LeBorgne, W., Lee, L. Stemple, J., & Bush, H., (2009). Perceptual findings on the Broadway belt voice. *Journal of Voice, 24*(6), 678–689.

DeSilva, B. (2016). A survey of the current state of contemporary commercial music (CCM) vocal pedagogy training at the graduate level. (Publication no. 10111351) [Doctor of Musical Arts Dissertation]. ProQuest.

Edwards, M. (2018). Why it's time to add CCM to your studio. In M. Hoch (Ed.), *So you want to sing CCM? (Contemporary Commercial Music): A guide for performers* (pp. 264–286). Rowman & Littlefield.

Edwin, R. (2005). Contemporary music theater: Louder than words. *Journal of Singing, 61*(3), 291–292.

Feder, S., & McGill, A. (2021). Diversity, equity, inclusion, and racial injustice in the classical music professions: A call to action. In M. Beckerman & P Boghossian (Eds.) *Classical music: Contemporary perspectives and challenges* (pp 87–102). Open Book Publishers.

Griffiths, A. (26 November, 2019). Playing the white man's tune: Inclusion in elite classical music. *British Journal of Music Education, 37*(1), 55–70. doi: 10.1017/S0265051719000391

Hoch, M. (2022). The postpandemic pedagogue. *Journal of Singing, 78*(4), 483–489. www.muse.jhu.edu/article/847973.

Kajikawa, L. (2019). The possessive investment in classical music: Confronting legacies of white supremacy in U.S. schools and departments of music. In K. W Krenshaw, L. C. Harris, D.M Hosang, and G. Lipsitz (Eds.), *Seeing race* again (1st edition, pp. 155–174). University of California Press. doi: 10.1525/9780520972148-008

King, M., & Nix, J. (2019). Conservatory teaching and learning. In G. Welch, D. Howard, & J. Nix (Eds.) *The Oxford handbook of singing* (pp. 689–705). Oxford University Press.

Meyer, D., Nix, J., Helding., L, Henderson, A., Carroll, T., Faust, J., & Peterson, C. Reentry following COVID-19: Concerns for singers. *Journal of Singing, 78*(2), 211–232. doi: 10.53830/VAPD6085

Miller, S. Nazaroff, W., Jiminez, J., Boerstra, A., Buonanna, G., Dancer, S., Kurnitski, J., Marr, L., Mowarska, L., & Noakes, C. (2021). Transmission of SARV-CoV-2 by inhalation of respiratory aerosol in the Skagit Valley Chorale superspreading event. *Indoor Air, 31*, 14–323. doi: 10.1111/ina.12751

Nielson, (2019). *Nielson mid-year report US 2019*. Retrieved from www.nielsen.com/wp-content/uploads/sites/3/2019/06/nielsen-us- music-mid-year-report-2019.pdf

Overland, C. (2016). Gender composition and salary of the music faculty in NASM Accredited universities: 2000–2014. *College Music Symposium: Exploring Diverse Perspectives*. doi: 10.18177/sym.2016.56.sr.11129

Pan American Health Organisation, (2021). *Gendered Health Analysis: Covid-19 in the Americas*. https://iris.paho.org/bitstream/handle/10665.2/55432/PAHOEGCCOVID-19210006_eng.pdf?sequence=4&isAllowed=y

Reinhert, K. (January 20, 2020). *Expanding the circle: CCM and popular music in higher ed*. https://singinginpopularmusics.com/2020/01/27/expanding-the-circle-ccm-and-popular-music-in-higher-ed/

Sergeant, D., & Himonides, E. (2022). Performing sex: The representation of male and female musicians in three performance genres. *Psychology of Music*, 1–38. doi: 10.1177/03057356221115458

Smith, G. D., & Powell, B. (2017). Welcome to the journal. *Journal of Popular Music Education, 1*(1), 3–8.

Smith, G. D., Powell, B., Fish, D. L., Kornfield, I., & Reinhert, K. (2018). Popular music education: A white paper by the Association for Popular

Music Education. *Journal of Popular Music Education*, 2(3), 298–298. doi: 10.1386/jpme.2.3.289_1

United Nations Entity for Gender Equality and the Empowerment of Women (UN Women) United Nations Secretariat, (9 April, 2020). *The impact of Covid-19 on women.* www.unwomen.org/sites/default/files/Headquarters/Attachments/Sections/Library/Publications/2020/Policy-brief-The-impact-of-COVID-19-on-women-en.pdf

Wicks, S. A. (January 9, 1998). *The monocultural perspective of music education.* The Chronicle of Higher Education. www.chronicle.com/article/the-monocultural-perspective-of-music-education/

Index

Note: Endnotes are indicated by the page number followed by "n" and the note number e.g., 14n29 refers to note 29 on page 14. Page numbers in **bold** refer to tables.

academic credentials 99, 149
academic employment 11, 80, 106, 109, 147; and advertisement 70, 78, 85, 109, 111, 120, 123–4
access: to academic employment 11, 12, 57, 105, 119, 123, 136, 147, 149; to academic journals 121; to musical theatre training 54, 55; to research participants 18, 47
accompanist 33–4
aesthetic 126; and CCM 82; and classical 84; 86, 94–5, 126, 143, 148; and musical theatre singing 82, 100; and voice pedagogy literature 21
ambiguity 98
amplification 43–4, 46, 60–1, 67, 102–3, 138
anonymise 19, 22, 56, 141
articulation 68; and CCM 5, 8, 39, 63–4
asset 102, 106, 108, 111; and classical academic training/performance 104–6, 108; and musical theatre performance 109, 111; and voice science credentials 107

audition 3, 40, 43, 66, 82, 138, 139; and audition book 37; and audition cuts 4; and academic entry 11, 14n29, 148
authority 28, 42, 87, 92, 127, 135, 136

belt 3, **5**, **6**, 36, 37, 46, 47n18, 51–3, 62–8, 73n53, 85, 93, 104, 122, 138, 139
bias 21, 47n8, 110, 120, 131; and gender 142
big Q research *see* qualitative
bodywork 35–6
Bourdieu 23, 25–6, 129, 149, 150; and capitals 100, 101, 106, 108, 111, 112; and doxa 122; and field 118; and habitus 89–90, 94, 98
breathing 35, 36, 69, 84, 85; and belt 65; and CCM **5–7**, 39, 64–5; and dance 45

capital: and cultural 101–4, 110, 112, 119, 130–1, 141; and educational 104–6, 130; and scientific 106–8, 101, 119–22, 135; and social 101, 106, 111–12, 119; and symbolic 89, 101, 106, 108–11, 119, 129

Index

chest register **5–9**, 39, 51, 53, 66, 67, 69, 72n44, 139
civility 126–9
conceptual framework 20, 21, 23–8, 122, 149, 150
constructionism 20
credibility 18, 22, 87, 106, 107, 127
cross training 37, 47n18, 86, 138

dance 34, 45–6, 64, 82, 104, 126, 130
data collection 18, 21, 23
deep structures 69, 70, 77–9, 83, 85, 87, 94, 128
diction 68, 86, 87, 123, 124
disciplines 25, 26, 27, 100, 110, 129; classical 103; music 106, 147; musical theatre 63, 70, 92, 100, 102; voice pedagogy 10, 17, 20, 91, 150
discouragement 56
dispositions 90, 96, 97, 100, 106, 108
diversity 92
doxa 122–3, 126

effectiveness 17, 18, 47
embodiment 45, 63, 79, 83–5, 90, 96–8, 102–4
employability 53
enculturate 94, 97
epistemology 20–1
ethnicity 90, 92–3, 97
evidence-based pedagogy 107
excluded 25, 27, 95, 96, 105, 120, 123, 124, 126, 135
exclusion *see* excluded
expertise 53, 56, 60, 70, 71, 80, 85–6, 107, 119; lack of 122

family background 96–7
field 25–8, 89, 96, 98, 99, 101, 111–12; of academic teaching 57, 99, 105, 110, of higher music education 2, 147; 141–3; of musical theatre 100; and reproduction 134–6; of voice pedagogy 12, 16, 22, 54, 98, 99, 102, 104–9; 111, 118–32, 140, 149–50
field research 17, 19, 22–3
foreign language 37, 38, 46, 87, 138
functional training 35, 53, 85, 138

game 118, 122; of voice pedagogy 28, 120, 122, 135, 142
gender 90–2, 97, 113n8, 113n17, 136–7, 147
graduate programmes 11, 13n29, 42, 112, 146
group classes 40

habitus 23, 25–7, 89–100, 106, 112, 118, 119, 129–30, 150
hierarchy 26, 44, 106, 119, 121, 132, 147, 150n5
Higher Music Education *see* HME
HME 2, 3, 10–11, 12, 34, 52, 55, 70, 71, 77, 78, 92, 110, 136

idiosyncratic *see* idiosyncrasy
idiosyncrasy 34–6, 77, 100, 46
implicit structures 23, 25–6, 34, 36, 84, 85, 100, 135
insider 18, 22
interpretive framework *see* conceptual framework
interviews 18–19, 21–5, 45, 50, 54, 78, 84, 97, 140, 141

legit 3, 37, 46, 47n18, 50, 52, 54, 67, 78, 80, 83, 130, 131
lessons: content 16, 17, 25, 25, 34–46, 137
legitimacy 1, 27, 99, 101, 103, 105–7, 123, 132, 137
legitimised *see* legitimacy
lineage 19, 135, 136
linguistic 86, 123–4, 126, 135

master-apprentice 10, 19, 77, 91
microphone *see* amplification
multi-sited focused ethnography 22–5, 141

Index 157

NASM 41–2
NAST 42
National Association of Schools of Music *see* NASM
National Association of Schools of Theatre *see* NAST
national tour 3, 79, 81, 83, 102, 106, 108, 112, 119, 120
networking *see* networks
networks 19, 22, 106, 111, 112, 118

observation 12, 17, 19, 22–4, 36, 43, 55, 134
ontological position 20

participant observation 23, 53, 84
performance background 11, 17, 78, 81, 84, 87, 108, 123, 140; as a music director 80; as symbolic capital 108, 111
power 1, 28, 44, 54, 91, 118, 119–21, 126, 127, 129, 132n13, 135, 142
power dynamic 56, 91, 141
prejudice 131, 47n8
privilege 1, 136, 142

qualifications 11, 17, 18, 34, 51, 52, 54, 55, 70, 99, 102, 105, 110–12, 123, 124, 126, 127, 136, 146
qualitative 19–23

reciprocity 23, 53
reflexive thematic analysis 23, 27
relational 18, 118
relationships 25, 102, 129, 142
repertoire 34–9, 46, 47n7, 85, 138–40; CCM 4, 39–43, 58, 60, 70, 99, 145; classical 11, 37, 83, 86–7, 102–4, 138, 139; musical theatre 3, 11, 34–7, 102, 109, 138; and taste 100, 104
research design 16, 21–3
research questions 17, 21, 25, 140, 141

scales 34, 39
Shulman, L. 28, 34
signature pedagogies 23–8, 33, 34, 36, 122
social networking 102
social space 96, 100, 101, 105, 118, 129, 135, 136
social structure 25–8, 82, 95, 98, 122, 135, 136
sound system *see* amplification
speech **5**, **8**, 39, 46, 65, 66, 68, 104, 107, 121
stretching 35, 36
studio spaces 34
style elements 5
surface structures 25, 33, 34, 104, 114n43
symbolic power 122–9

taste 1, 27, 89, 100, 104
teacher training 53, 110
teaching approaches 35, 36, 46
teaching location 34
teaching skill 86, 109, 111
technique: CCM 39, 138; classical 4, 38, 39, 54, 55, 70, 83, 138
theory 21, 23, 25, 26, 64
training background 50, 78, 80, 93
training opportunity 53, 130, 140
triple threat 41, 82
trust 18, 28n11

validation 10, 19, 120, 135, 146, 150
versatility 2, 127
vocal damage 10, 63, 139
voice pedagogy programmes 10, 11, 149
voice science 55, 63, 64, 68, 107, 108, 119–21

warm up 35, 46
white 92, 121, 130, 148
white supremacy 93

For Product Safety Concerns and Information please contact our EU representative GPSR@taylorandfrancis.com
Taylor & Francis Verlag GmbH, Kaufingerstraße 24, 80331 München, Germany

www.ingramcontent.com/pod-product-compliance
Lightning Source LLC
Chambersburg PA
CBHW051747230426
43670CB00012B/2198